To: Mr.
Thanks for all
your prayers & support.
Appreciate all you do
for FCA.
May GOD BLESS YOU
& YOURS!

Johnny
Dyess

Matthew 17:20-21

NEW SET OF DOWNS

HOW
JOHNNY DYESS
FOUGHT OFF HIS
GREATEST WOULD-BE
TACKLER AND
RETURNED TO
WINNING WAYS

BY **KYLE MOOTY**

TABLE OF CONTENTS

ACKNOWLEDGEMENTS

FIRST, I WANT to thank Johnny Dyess. He is a great example of no matter how caught up you seem to be in life's downward spiral, there is a ladder to escape.

My mother… I could try and write some words but they'll never express how truly blessed I have been being her son.

And though I'm not sure what I did to deserve more blessings, God gave me two of the greatest daughters.

Oh, and I have siblings that are second to none.

Ricky Adams, thanks for helping me finally get this book, as they say, "out the door."

Friends? I've got a few scattered around the country. I wouldn't trade any of them. Some have moved on to a better place, but while on earth they taught me how to better live here. Some still here have played a major role in helping me get this book completed.

To those aforementioned who have supported me regardless of whether or not I landed with my feet firmly planted, I believe, have understood why I continuously bounced around as I searched for the ever-elusive greener pasture.

Foreword

By MARLIN "SCOOTER" DYESS

Dyess family photo
Marlin "Scooter" Dyess

JOHNNY DYESS IS my nephew.

Johnny grew up in Elba, Alabama, same as I had. He attended and graduated from Elba High School in 1978, same as I had in 1956. He was always a dedicated person to whatever he was involved in doing. He was a good student, athlete, family oriented and involved in his church activities; had a very successful football and academic career during his high school days.

He had a burning desire to attend the University of Alabama and play for Coach Bryant. He got the opportunity to walk on and he took it; spent four years with the Crimson Tide and was on the National Championship teams of 1978 and '79. Some of best things that go along with this "team concept" is the friendship you build for a lifetime with the guys.

Everything always starts at home and he had great parents and a fine brother as they grew up. He was taught the work ethic both at home and in college. I still can remember Coach Bryant stressing, "Character is not measured by how hard we get knocked, but how well we get up."

Johnny was always a respectful person to other people. It is a pleasure to say a few words about someone who made a bad decision (haven't we all) in life and then to come to Jesus who is the Savior to us all.

We need Jesus and each other!

Marlin "Scooter" Dyess
Captain of 1959-60 University of Alabama Football Team

INTRODUCTION

JOHNNY DYESS WILL trust you like no one unless he has a reason not to trust you. He is lovingly cautious that way. Has to be; he's come too far to put himself in a bad situation again.

Johnny will be the first to tell you he did just about everything imaginable to throw away the good sense God and his parents provided him. He was raised right, raised in a church, raised by good people, salt-of-the-earth type folks.

He loved sports, was pretty dang good in baseball and was especially good in football in his hometown of Elba, Alabama.

Like any teenager, there were opportunities for Johnny to explore the mischievous side of life…. which he did. But by the time he followed his childhood dream of playing football at the University of Alabama for its legendary head coach Paul "Bear" Bryant, he had managed to stay at least as clean as the rest of those wearing the Crimson Tide uniform. He might have a beer or two on occasion during the off-season, but there was no time or reason to mess up the good thing he had going during his four years as a walk-on at Bama. National championships his first two seasons there only made him love what he was doing all the more.

He was carrying the banner not only for the good folks of Elba, but also the family name. Uncle Marlin "Scooter" Dyess had been something of a star for the Bama boys decades earlier when Bryant first arrived in Tuscaloosa.

Now and then, during those brief moments around Bryant when Dyess and his teammates weren't sweating profusely as they willed themselves to out-work their opponents, Bryant would ask Johnny how Marlin was doing, as well as Johnny's parents, Percy and Clara Ann.

Everyone was fine, Johnny assured Bryant, but during his post-Crimson Tide days, Johnny was the one whose actions brought concern to other folks.

He returned to Elba, which offered little more than a steady job working at a factory. He'd move up the ladder, thanks to the strong work ethic instilled in him by Percy and Clara Ann, and of course, Bryant. He would make contacts with good people that were able to help him climb the ladder, but soon Johnny found himself beneath the bottom rung as he surrounded himself with people that had everything but his best in their hearts.

Life became dark. In fact, it became too dark for Johnny to notice.

Years into a drug culture that cost him everything from a good job to a loving wife and stepdaughter, not to mention respect he once enjoyed throughout his community, Johnny fell into a drug culture that came oh so close to taking his life, and certainly threatened his freedom.

Somehow, after more encounters with the devil than most people can endure, Johnny was shown the light. Finally, he worked to stay there. Finally, Johnny was living again, this time better – no, much better – than before.

Johnny now shares his testimony in hopes of saving people from following his previous paths. *New Set of Downs* lays out where he came from, what he became, how Johnny managed to lose it all and eventually escape from the dark and return to a light brighter than ever.

PROLOGUE

JOHNNY DYESS LOST his third game as a high school freshman at Elba to nearby Opp, and that year his Tigers finished with as many losses, five, as they did wins. In fact, during his four years playing at Elba High School, Johnny's teams never finished better than 6-4. So, when Alabama lost its third game during his freshman walk-on season to Southern California, let's just say Johnny knew how to handle it. He wouldn't have to fall back on such experiences often as a member of the Crimson Tide.

At this point, Johnny had a good handle on his life, too. He even returned to his hometown as a two-time national champion at Alabama, and later worked his way up to a good job at a local factory. He found a good woman to marry and gained a wonderful stepdaughter he was as proud of as if she had come from his own genes.

Johnny did not have to experience losing much during his Crimson Tide career. Alabama would go 42-5-1 during his time under the guidance of Paul "Bear" Bryant, winning those national championships as a freshman and sophomore.

Of course, as a walk on, Johnny was akin to a grunt in the military, used as a punching bag for starters and even coaches, especially when things didn't go well on Saturdays. Per usual, Johnny would handle those moments, too.

Always a man of faith, Johnny learned to truly dread Sundays following a rare Alabama loss. That's when his Alabama coaches would take out their frustrations on the team, and not wanting to get the starters and more highly recruited players injured, the walk-ons took the brunt of the punishment, even if it had been poor play by the starters in the loss in the first place.

Johnny's freshman year at Alabama would include wins over Nebraska, Missouri, Washington, Florida, Tennessee, Virginia Tech, LSU and archrival Auburn en route to receiving a berth in the Sugar Bowl as the champion of the Southeastern Conference. The Crimson Tide were ranked No. 2 nationally. No. 1 was Penn State, and its head coach, Joe Paterno, elected to turn down the Orange Bowl in hopes of securing the school's first national title by leaving nothing to chance if his team could beat Alabama. The heavyweight championship bout had been held at the same location just 109 days earlier, but the 15-round fight between Muhammad Ali and Leon Spinks had nothing on the slugfest that was about to go down in the Louisiana Superdome.

It was a cold and rainy day outside on New Year's Day, 1979. Inside, it was warm and dry, and thanks to two of the nation's finest defenses, it was about to get hot.

Alabama was led by running back Tony Nathan (of the movie *Woodlawn* fame). The Tide quarterback was Jeff Rutledge. Penn State had its own stars on offense, including quarterback Chuck Fusina, wide receiver Scott Fitzkee, and place-kicker Matt Bahr. It also had a pair of offensive linemen – Keith Dorney and Eric Cunningham – that would be taken high in the NFL Draft. In fact, 20 players participating in that game would go on to NFL careers.

Defense ruled this day. It was a gut check of a game. Both teams had trouble moving the ball, but Alabama did manage a touchdown pass from Rutledge to Bruce Bolton late in the first half for a 7-0 lead.

Penn State tied the game on a Fusina-to-Fitzkee TD pass, but thanks to a 62-yard punt return by Lou Ikner, followed by a Major Ogilvie touchdown run three plays later, Alabama held a 14-7 lead as Penn State faced a crucial fourth-quarter drive.

A poor pitch by Rutledge forced by Penn State's Matt Millen had given the Nittany Lions hope as they recovered at the Alabama 19. Fullback Matt Suhey gained 11 to the 8-yard line on the first play from scrimmage. The Lions gained 2 yards on the next first down. On second down from the 6, Fusina found Fitzkee on a short pass. Fitzkee appeared to have a clear path to the end zone, but Bama's Don McNeil sprinted up and hammered Fitzkee out of bounds inside the 1-yard line.

"McNeil; that was the ballgame," Johnny said of the crucial tackle on Fitzkee. "If he doesn't make that tackle, we've got to drive it and score."

Johnny didn't dress out for that historic Sugar Bowl; instead, he sat in the stands in New Orleans with friends. He watched as intently as if he were one of the Bama boys lining up on the goal line.

On third down, Suhey tried diving over the top of the Alabama defense, but he was stopped short by a host of Tide defenders. That brought up fourth down, a play that would go down as one of the most legendary in bowl game history.

During a timeout, Fusina had asked an official, "How much is it?" Alabama All-American defensive lineman Marty Lyons looked at the Penn State quarterback and said, "About that much," spreading his fingers apart to indicate the distance.

"Ten inches?" Fusina asked.

"Yeah," Lyons responded. "You better pass."

Fusina should have heeded those words. Paterno reportedly wanted to call a play-action pass, but was talked out of it by his assistant coaches.

On fourth down with 6:49 remaining, less than a foot away from the end zone, Penn State's 19-game win streak was on the line, as well as a shot at the school's first national title.

Then-Arkansas Athletic Director Frank Broyles, who was the color commentator, alongside Keith Jackson, during the ABC broadcast, said moments after the game that he hated to see anybody lose such a football game.

Penn State had made its decision. The play call was for tailback

Matt Guman to make the required distance, a matter of inches, into the heart of the Alabama defense. All-American linebacker Barry Krauss and cornerback Mike Clements were waiting and stopped Guman in his tracks shy of the goal line.

Krauss suffered temporary paralysis on the play, as well as a chronic pinched nerve in his neck. He had hit Guman so hard it loosened the rivets on his helmet.

"Everybody talks about the goal-line stand, but it wasn't over then," Johnny said. "We had to punt to 'em." The Tide stopped Penn State again and would go on to win the national title.

The stars at Alabama were plentiful – Nathan, Rutledge, Ogilvie, Lyons, Krause, Wayne Hamilton, E.J. Junior III, Curtis McGriff, David Hannah, Ikner, Dwight Stephenson, Jim Bunch, Buddy Aydelette, Byron Bragg and McNeal.

Idols or not, Johnny saw them almost daily in practice, and being a walk-on was not fun at times as they were used as live dummies by the coaches. "They were rough on us," Johnny said.

Johnny was, if possible, hooked on the Crimson Tide more than ever, even though his time was spent mainly as a special team's player on Saturdays – he had four carries for seven yards during his career at Alabama.

Winning, especially at his beloved Alabama, was an unquenchable high.

A few years later, Johnny would be out of football. Where would he feel such a sensation again? Would he ever feel the ecstasy of such great on-the-field moments again?

He had no idea.

Johnny handled much of his post-Crimson Tide days well, returning home to a good job that he turned into an even better one. Bad decisions had not been Johnny's yardstick.

Seemingly overnight, but what was a lengthy, downward spiral, Johnny found himself behind a meth pipe. What had begun as a bad decision would soon become an even worse habit.

The night had fallen on Johnny. Things would become even darker for him… much darker.

Move forward to September 11, 2012, and Johnny was a spectator in the stands when his uncle, former Alabama star Marlin "Scooter" Dyess, was honored at halftime of a Crimson Tide game alongside Johnny's childhood idol, Johnny Musso. Dyess, was honored at halftime of a Crimson Tide game alongside Johnny's childhood idol, Johnny Musso.

Johnny Dyess probably couldn't have walked into the stadium that day had he still carried the burden of methamphetamine with him. There simply was not an entrance that big. However, by this point, Johnny was making quite a stand of his own.

Chapter 1

RED-HORNED TRAVEL AGENT

IF LIFE HAD a basement, Johnny Dyess was sitting in its recliner. Yes, he was still alive, but after all he had been afforded in life, he'd found himself at rock bottom. If he realized as much, Johnny wasn't in any hurry to make any lifestyle changes.

Had he only made a list of pros and cons, you know, the ones a mother will suggest when trying to decide on things of the utmost importance for a young child, such as taking that summer trip to Six Flags with cousins or staying to play out the Little League season with teammates. Had Johnny done so, perhaps he would have realized the cons far outweighed the pros when he sought the answer for his mid-life crisis.

Ever catch yourself looking back, realizing after the fact, perhaps even several years later, that what you once had *was* the good life? Maybe you even thought those were the days you had it all. Johnny once had it all.

No, there was no new hot rod waiting in the driveway for him to drive to college. Johnny did get a nice car for his senior year of high school, but he would soon destroy it. He didn't have all the new gadgets to impress his friends, particularly the girls, but what he had was good.

He was a small-town football star with legendary bloodlines that saw him play for four years for an even more legendary figure, University of Alabama football coach Paul William "Bear" Bryant. Things were especially good during those years.

After the glory days were behind him, Johnny opted for another wondrous feeling, one that would leave him happy, even if numb to the world around him. He became engrained in a drug culture, albeit as a loner more so than a social user.

Some may say Johnny was born under a really bad sign, a Friday the 13th – Nov. 13, 1959. But, he wasn't.

Looking back, he pretty much had all the ingredients necessary for a good-life recipe. He had great parents, he succeeded in school, and he had a powerful heart in his chest that made him produce numbers on the football field a guy twice his physique would envy. In fact, today, Johnny will tell you he was indeed one of the lucky ones.

He may have caused a nightmare for himself and those around him, but Johnny survived the ordeal as, sadly, too few others have.

Ironic thing about drug users, they care so much for drugs that cares so little for them. Oh sure, drugs give a faux rush to their victims, letting them enjoy brief periods without clarity, which is precisely what they seek; blurred thoughts where nothing makes sense, yet in their distorted minds, everything does.

Drugs eventually steal users' pride, dignity and whatever quality of life they once enjoyed. And, it gets worse. Meth takes away dreams, goals, family and friends, as well as teeth, tone and general health. Little things that were once important, such as personal hygiene and a clean place to live… forget about it. Those things take a backseat to seeking that next high.

Johnny hid his problem as best he could, although many times, when he thought he'd beaten the system, he was the one who had suffered the beating. He just didn't realize it.

Getting high led to Johnny's lowest of lows.

His personal voyage to the heights of an amateur football player –

he was a member of two national championships during his four years at the University of Alabama – was followed by a visit to depths only a life of drugs could help him plunge into. It was a hell no football practice, regardless of how long and how bruising, could match.

Before Johnny could climb out of that hell, there were some embarrassing moments, life-threatening moments, and moments that shaped him into who he is today.

Satan saw to it. Johnny was given carte blanche, an all-access ticket by Satan to hell. Johnny knew where the hideaway key was to the elevator down there. He would be a guest of The Devil… often.

Today, Johnny acknowledges the multiple bad choices he made that led him to the most humbling of moments. He remembers well the date: Wednesday, July 29, 2009, and it was about 3 p.m. when angels came for him in the form of dark vehicles, SUVs, if you will.

Also, today he understands that all things Auburn are not bad. It took a mighty power to convince the dyed-in-the-wool Alabama fan to acknowledge such. If you grew up on the side of Alabama's greatest rivalry as Johnny, perhaps you can understand his saying anything positive about his rival takes involvement of a higher power.

Johnny had faith. He had talent and a will to overcome whatever shortcomings he had been dealt. For God's sake, he even had a loyal dog.

Somewhere along the way, Johnny's course in life took the proverbial, wrong fork in the road. When he had travelled so far down it he became lost, far more than even he realized. He was so misplaced in a world that had been laid out nicely for him, that the days of serving God changed to days of standing guard with an automatic rifle at a drug buy in a big city that may just as well have been a continent away. He carried the gun just in case the guy he was with, a friend only because of the guy's ability to obtain grade-A methamphetamine, suddenly needed protection in case their drug deal went awry.

Somehow, Johnny maintained a bit of cleanliness. He was not the stereotypical meth addict because he kept his weight up, making himself eat daily. He figured that way no one would notice. But the meth habit became a daily ritual, sometimes 24 hours bleeding over into the next day, or even the day after that.

Perhaps Johnny knew his parents would always be there. Perhaps he knew God would always welcome him at His house no matter which off-the-beaten path he had taken to arrive. He knew his dog would be around, even if a wife and beloved stepdaughter wouldn't. As it turns out, his guesses were correct.

Meth took the former high school star and Crimson Tide player to more fourth-and-longs than he ever faced on the gridiron. Meth took Johnny to the unemployment line. It took him to the inner drug world of Atlanta. And right on cue, it took him to jail… many times. Johnny knew the route there as well as the jailers

Meth took him to shameful moments he never imagined in his worst nightmares, such as the time it took him to a visit at jail in shackles to see his parents. It took him to New York's Times Square, though it was hardly the glitter-filled showcase Dick Clark presented us each New Year's Eve. And, God must have a great sense of humor because, lo and behold, it took him right next door to his most bitter rival before, during and after his playing days – Auburn University.

Fans of the hated Auburn Tigers, who wore what he considered to be a sickening combination of orange and blue, saw only the true potential in Johnny, and with the help of a higher power, they lifted him from the depths of a hell not many get to escape.

Though he didn't realize it at the time, God was Johnny's lead blocker on his life's fourth-and-goal and He gave enough of a push to get Johnny a new set of downs… and teeth.

This go-round in life, Johnny is honoring the most legendary of coaches, Jesus, and together they are unbeaten. Don't believe it? Ask meth. They've kicked its ass real good. "Bear" Bryant would be proud.

Chapter 2

ELBA, ALABAMA

Courtesy Marlin Dyess
Marlin Dyess turned down an offer to play football at Georgia Tech
to instead become a member of the Alabama Crimson Tide.

COFFEE COUNTY LAKE is just northwest of Elba. Fed mainly by Coon Creek, the lake produced some nice fish for locals to feast upon during its heyday. Also nearby is the Pea River, which has more varieties of fish but often proves more of a challenge. The river gets its name from its greenish color, and stones along the bank become extremely slippery when wet.

Johnny and his school-aged friends would often go fishing – "We were just old country boys" – at either the county lake or the local river.

"The big thing back then was to catch something big enough to go to Farmer's Bait Shop in Elba and get your picture taken," he recalled. Farmer's sold crickets and worms, and on multiple occasions Johnny and his friends were pictured in the local newspaper, the *Elba Clipper*, proudly posing with their large stringer from a day on the water.

Of course, having the river so close to the town's eastern side meant far more trouble at times than its slippery banks.

Floods have distressed the small town of Elba on multiple occasions, trying their best to deface its Norman Rockwell setting. There were levees added to protect the town from the river, but even those couldn't stop rising waters from crashing into the community when they chose to flood.

Nestled in Southeast Alabama in a region known as the Wiregrass, Elba is technically the county seat of Coffee County, which today has two courthouses, the original in Elba and one in the much larger town of nearby Enterprise, which has a population today about seven times larger than Elba.

Elba began as a gathering of individuals near a ferry that crossed the Pea River. Originally called Bridgeville, a contest was later held to name the town. One resident had been reading about the exploits of former French Emperor Napoleon Bonaparte, and how he had been exiled to the Mediterranean island of Elba in 1814. Someone thought that was good enough for the Alabama community. So, Elba was chosen as the town's official name, becoming incorporated in April 1853.

In March 1865, Elba was hard hit by a flood one month before the assassination of President Abraham Lincoln. The flood became known as "Lincoln Flood," which wreaked havoc on the town. It would hardly be the last one.

The March 1929 flood of Elba forced the completely inundated town to receive supplies dropped from airplanes. A levee was built around the town the next year. Nevertheless, floods came again – 1938, 1959 and 1975.

The worst was still to come.

In 1990, the Pea River near the downtown area crested at about 48 feet, damaging 130 of the 140 businesses in the community. Elba was flooded for four days. It was almost too much, but the town somehow survived. Smaller floods would come in 1994 and 1998.

Talk to anyone in Elba and they will confirm what a Google search of the town suggests: You can't talk about Elba's history without mentioning the various disasters.

In late 2002, repairs began on the levee to prevent future floods.

Johnny grew up on the north side of Elba in his parent's two-story home, situated between the Pea River and Whitewater Creek, the latter of which was as wide as many rivers. The Dyess' home flooded twice.

Johnny remembers his family having to live for a while with his second cousins after one flood. When they did return to their house they had to live upstairs. The parents stayed in one bedroom, while Johnny and his younger brother stayed in the other. They made a kitchen in the upstairs hallway, which sufficed during several months of remodeling the downstairs.

It was 1990, and Johnny was in the middle of his heavy-drinking days post-Alabama and pre-marriage. He was also dabbling in marijuana. He said he tried to keep it from the family, but he knows the chances are they became aware anyway.

Living quarters after the flood were just too close. "It was too long, I know that," Johnny said of the time he shared a bedroom with his younger brother. "But, I just did it. I didn't worry about it, I guess. I stayed out late, but I certainly didn't always hide it good enough because I got caught. They'd fuss about it, but I pretty much did what I wanted to do."

Elba's most famous native was former Alabama Governor James Elisha Folsom, better known as "Big Jim." At 6-foot, 8-inches, the origin of his moniker was obvious. He was released by the U.S. Army after a brief stint during World War II because he was simply too tall.

Folsom left college in 1929 to assist his hometown following that year's flood. He drifted about as a merchant sailor, a sparring partner in boxing rings, and as a doorman at a New York theater.

Folsom presided over Alabama as its governor from 1947-51 and again from 1956-59, becoming among the first southern governors to embrace integration. He said he was the little man's "big friend." He once told a crowd, "I plead guilty to stealing. I stole for you and you and you." During his Christmas message in 1949, Folsom said, "As long as the Negroes are held down by deprivation and lack of opportunity, the other poor people will be held down alongside them." He was also known as an anti-Prohibitionist, and was labeled the "wet candidate."

Folsom was as colorful as they came on the campaign circuit, entertaining crowds with country music and comedy. He campaigned in 1946 with a hillbilly band and brandished a mop and bucket, saying he would "clean out" the state capitol in Montgomery.

Folsom had married a judge's daughter in 1936, but after having two children, his wife, Sarah, died from complications related to pregnancy. In 1948, one year into his term as governor, Folsom had a paternity lawsuit filed against him by a former hotel cashier whom he'd met in Birmingham. She had a 22-month-old son at the time. Unfazed, Folsom was seen just days after the suit was filed kissing hundreds of models at New York City's Barbizon Modeling School, which had voted him "Number One Leap Year Bachelor." The suit was eventually dropped following a cash settlement from Folsom. Years later, Big Jim admitted he was indeed the child's father.

Also in 1948, the 39-year-old Folsom married a 20-year-old

secretary – Janelle – from the Alabama State Highway Department. They would have seven children.

Folsom would run for a third term as governor in 1962, but was defeated by George C. Wallace. During that campaign, Folsom had a live television appearance in which he appeared heavily intoxicated and could not remember the names of his own children. His physician speculated he may have suffered a stroke.

Folsom lost again in 1966 to Wallace's wife, Lurleen. To add insult to injury, Folsom's niece, Cornelia, would become George Wallace's second wife.

People around Coffee County still recall seeing "Big Jim" on the sidewalks on a hot summer day, taking off his socks and shoes seated on steps to a business and wiggling his toes so they would dry. He almost always wore white linen suits.

In the book "They Love a Man in the Country," one of Folsom's sisters, Ruby, was interviewed regarding Wallace, Big Jim's one-time protégé. The book quoted Ruby as saying Wallace "was titty high." Interviewed by a television station at an Enterprise nursing home just before her death, Ruby corrected the book's author, saying, "I didn't say he was titty high. I said he was about titty high."

Elba nor Coffee County has produced a governor since Folsom left office. The flooding has also been kept to a minimum in the 21st century.

During Folsom's second term as governor, the state of Alabama had a new powerful man calling shots, Paul "Bear" Bryant and his University of Alabama football team. Bryant's first team in 1958 included Marlin Dyess, an Elba product who would shine under the mentoring of his new coach.

Marlin Dyess had grown up on a small farm with four brothers and a sister.

Football is still huge in Elba on Friday nights. Blacks and whites, haves and have-nots, come together and cheer for their Tigers. The team carried a perfect record into the 2014 Class 2A state championship game before losing a second-quarter lead and falling short in its bid for a seventh state crown. Johnny Lamar Dyess, an Elba assistant, coached that game from the press box with a heavy heart as his father passed away one day earlier.

The Tigers returned to the championship game the next year to face the same opponent from Northeast Alabama, Fyffe High School. This time, Elba won that seventh state title.

Johnny is still coaching at his high school alma mater. Aside from the X's and O's of football, he is head junior varsity baseball coach, assistant varsity baseball coach, and cuts grass on school grounds.

Johnny attends Bible study regularly and is a deacon in the same church he grew up attending.

He guides his players through much more than how to hit the hole as a running back, or to read a quarterback's tendencies as a defensive back. He knows no problem, no flood, is too great to overcome and he has the ultimate in connections to young men's struggles.

Johnny knows miracles can happen. He is more than glad to introduce his "connection" today to anyone who has yet to be formally introduced. As he discovered when he faced his greatest adversity, his "connection" is always there for him.

CHAPTER 3

A TIME TO PUSH

PLAYING IN HIS backyard, often by himself, Johnny was a star. He would throw the ball to himself or to anyone or anything that would return it when he threw it, even if it meant bouncing it against a wall. This was the case regardless of what type of ball he was using... baseball, football or basketball.

His first chance at organized baseball would give him a chance to show others his skills.

On the drive to the Little League draft, Wilson Percy Dyess warned his 9-year-old son about one particular position he did not want Johnny playing: "Son, remember you can play anywhere you want to, but don't get behind that plate."

Catching is the most physical position in baseball and Percy would rather his son not be subjected to foul tips and bounced baseballs hitting him almost nonstop.

Percy dropped off his son and drove away, planning to come back in plenty of time to retrieve him by the end of the baseball festivities.

Before the kids took the field, there had to be a draft for the coaches to choose their prospects. Elkin Williamson, one of the coaches, chose

Johnny to play on his team. After all the players were selected, Williamson asked the youngsters which position they wanted to play. Johnny didn't hesitate and walked over by those who wanted to pitch. After all, that's the position he had always fancied himself in his backyard.

Williamson took his players straight to their first practice on the Elba School grounds.

After hitting some grounders and fly balls, Williamson had the players break off to their desired positions to begin batting practice. Johnny was among the kids standing near the mound, in hopes he'd really be a pitcher.

The player who had elected to be a catcher struggled from the very first pitch. "He wasn't catching anything," Johnny said. "Coach was getting real frustrated. It was taking forever. The catcher would have to run to the backstop and get the ball after every pitch."

Johnny noticed the catcher had on all of this gear, chest protector, shin guards, mask and even a most unique glove called a mitt.

"Catching had all that equipment and was very involved in every play," Johnny said. "Man, I thought catching had all that going on."

Catcher's equipment has been referred to as "tools of ignorance."

Nevertheless, when Williamson asked Johnny if he could catch, hoping some player, anyone, could speed things up, Johnny was quick to grab the equipment. It proved to be a very wise move by Williamson. "No balls were getting by me," Johnny said.

Practice was winding down when Johnny, still behind the plate, noticed his father's truck pulling around one of the school buildings and up to practice. He would exit the truck, walk around to its front, and watch the reminder of practice leaning against it

Being the catcher, Johnny was the last to take batting practice.

"I was no more than knee-high to a duck but I was knocking the ball everywhere," Johnny said. "After the practice, the coach told my daddy, 'Percy, I have found me a catcher.' Of course, I was still so excited because I had hit the ball so well and the coach had nothing but great things to say about me catching."

Johnny remained excited all the way home. When they arrived, Percy told Johnny, "Go in the bedroom."

"That ain't never good," Johnny recalled. "He came in and said, 'You know why we are in here, don't you?' I said, 'Because I did what you told me not to do.'"

Johnny's enthusiasm had come down a notch or two, and Percy now had his son's full attention. Nevertheless, just as Johnny was beginning to feel ashamed for going against his father's wishes, Percy looked at his son and said, "Now, be the best catcher you can be."

Johnny would become an all-star catcher for most of his baseball-playing days.

Chapter 4

NOT FALLING FOR THAT

JOHNNY HAD TASTED success and understood he was simply better playing football than others his age during backyard clashes, ones where he often emulated Alabama great Johnny Musso.

Elba finally got its first organized youth football program when Johnny was a third grader. There were two teams, the Black and the Gold. Coaches Russell Cash and Doug Martin divided the players, and Cash chose Johnny, a draft gem at the time.

The teams would practice against one another, and on a couple of occasions during the year, play an actual game.

Cash made Johnny a star, centering his offense around the young running back, who was difficult to stop for other players his age. After all, he had been playing backyard ball against many older guys. Not only did Cash's squad never lose, there was never much of a contest with Johnny running the ball.

Johnny was very impressionable, and admitted he really like Cash. He was so fond of his coach, in fact, that for one year, or at least a portion of a football season, Johnny became an Auburn fan.

Cash was a big Auburn fan, having graduated from the

university and having prime season tickets to Tigers' games at Jordan-Hare Stadium.

"He brainwashed me," Johnny laughed. "The next year we were the Rams and we wore blue. He had two sons, one was a year younger than me and the other was a year older than me. They'd take me to one Auburn game each year. I even got caught up in that Pat Sullivan for Heisman hype. I wasn't really for 'em, but I did have an Auburn jersey."

Sullivan won the Heisman Trophy in 1971, despite being all but shut down in the final regular season game against Alabama, 31-7, in the Iron Bowl.

Cash's influence and free trips to Auburn games almost worked, but in 1972 Auburn blocked two punts and returned both for late touchdowns as the Tigers rallied for a stunning, 17-16 victory over the Crimson Tide in a game that became known as the 'Punt Bama Punt' Iron Bowl on Dec. 2, at Birmingham's Legion Field. Johnny, though young, returned to his roots.

"When Auburn beat Alabama, I just told him, 'Coach Cash, I'm sorry, but the only way you can beat Alabama is by blocking two punts,'" Johnny recalled.

And that was it. Johnny was back in full allegiance with the Crimson Tide.

Cash had tickets at Auburn games on the 50-yard line, but Johnny was happier seeing Alabama with his parents while sitting in the end zone at Tuscaloosa. "I didn't care," Johnny said. "I just wanted to be there. "

Percy and Clara Ann gave Johnny the full experience of Alabama games, usually going each year to homecoming where he could watch the parade, then walking over the Denny Chimes, where captains of past Crimson Tide football teams had placed their hands and footprints in concrete on the sidewalks.

His uncle "Scooter's" prints were placed there in 1959. Johnny's favorite, however, may have been the 1965 marks left by former UA legend Joe Namath. "Namath was a big deal and I couldn't wait to get up there and see his footprints," Johnny said. "His footprints were a little different than anybody else because he was the first to have molded cleats when everyone else had screw-ons. Of course, I wanted his white shoes, too."

During his days as a college football commentator, the late Frank Broyles said football was simply different in Alabama.

"The people of Alabama believe in football," Broyles said. "It's a part of their life. When you're born in Alabama, you're either an Alabama fan or Auburn fan."

Free tickets could not sway young Johnny. He was sold on Alabama football. He believed in it. Still does.

Chapter 5

31 TRAP

Dyess family photo
Johnny Dyess was always as tough as nails while running
the ball for the Elba Tigers.

PERHAPS ELBA KNEW it had a future star as it began organized football – Little League – for third graders soon after Johnny walked onto the field. He was, after all, a Dyess, and he backed it up as the toughest kid on the field. He said his coach made a star out of him by giving him the ball in clutch situations. It wasn't like he had many to out-perform as there were just two teams – the Black and the Gold, the team colors of Elba High School.

"I didn't get a big head because I loved the game so much," he said. "I guess at an early age I understood football. My coach would let other people have the ball, but when it came to crunch time, he'd give it to me. I was always there for the big play. When the coaches said, 'Bread and butter,' it meant they were gonna pitch me the ball. Most of the time, I'd score."

When Johnny was little, his teams never lost, literally, and usually because of him. He was simply faster and tougher than the average kid, especially around Elba. That could have been a disadvantage since most of the time he found himself playing backyard ball against much larger boys… tackle… without pads. "I liked the contact. I wasn't scared," Johnny said. "And, I could run the ball. I had that knack, the instinct. And, I liked to block."

Johnny never experienced a loss as a member of a football team until he was in junior high school.

The town's local weekly newspaper, the *Elba Clipper*, profiled a player each week. On the week Johnny was listed, the *Clipper* wrote "Dyess hustles in practice and in the game. No matter what the score, Johnny Dyess will always be a winner."

Johnny was also not selfish, stating in his *Clipper* profile, "You must be willing to block if you want other players to block for you."

When the Elba Tigers needed a big play, they often followed the rule of thumb the Little League coaches had employed. There was no need to spread the field and throw deep. Just give the ball to their bread and butter.

On occasion, Johnny would break the huddle and line up at

fullback. If the opponent had somebody over center, the Tigers would audibilize to a play he favored more than any other, 31 Trap. When the defense obeyed, Johnny would shift to the right side of quarterback and follow that guard through the line.

"Most of the time, I was one-on-one with the linebacker or safety," he said. "If the play was executed right, it was a good play. But, if we ran it and it didn't work, it was a disaster."

Like many smaller schools, Elba didn't turn away ninth graders (freshmen) from its varsity if they could help the team. Johnny and a couple of his buddies fit the mold and suited up for the varsity. By the third game of his freshman season, Johnny found himself starting at cornerback. He saw some action at running back, too. He was especially busy during football season, playing on the junior high, B Team and varsity squads of the Tigers.

The older and more experienced Johnny became at running the ball, the more 31 Trap proved to be a good play. His best game came as a junior (1976 season) at home came against Opp, a town just to the west in Covington County. Opp is a larger school and Elba had only managed one touchdown against the Bobcats in the previous two seasons.

However, on this September night, Johnny would carry the ball 27 times for 195 yards in a 20-0 whipping of the Bobcats. "People still talk about that game," he said with a grin. "Their fans were kinda stunned."

A small back at 5-foot, 9-inches tall and 160 pounds, Johnny was surprisingly more of a power runner. It was obvious to the estimated crowd of 3,000 watching him against Opp that even as an underclassman Johnny had all the skills to continue the family tradition of football excellence at Elba High School. Others noticed too, as Johnny would be named an Honorable Mention All-State running back.

"Scooter" Dyess had been a star at Alabama during "Bear" Bryant's first two seasons leading his alma mater. "I never got to watch him play, but "Scooter" was always my idol growing up," Johnny said. "I had heard stories about how good he was and how good his teams were."

Elba has a strong football tradition for such a small town. It had won three mythical state championships in the pre-playoff era of the 1950s – '51, '54, and '55 – thanks in large part to "Scooter" Dyess, and the Tigers have won four state titles during the playoff era in 1989, 1992, 2011 and 2015.

Elba managed only a 4-5 record in Johnny's freshman year in 1974 under Coach Paul Bass, and the Tigers were 5-5 when he was a sophomore, playing for both Bass and Hinton Johns, who finished out the season as head coach.

Elba opened the 1975 season with a 1-2 record. Game four was at Opp. Randy Griffin, who had coached one season (1972) at Elba before bolting for Opp, led the Bobcats to a 26-7 pasting of the Tigers. That didn't sit well with Elba fans, who loudly booed Bass off the field.

Though the Tigers won their next two outings, Bass was basically run out of town. Why?

"We weren't very good, I guess," Johnny said. Johns finished out the season as the interim head coach, a move that played in Johnny's favor. The Tigers ran the veer formation, and Johns saw Johnny had the ability to run the football and run it with success.

Despite playing early and often, Johnny was rarely injured. There was, however, one exception. It came during his junior season at nearby Enterprise, a town that decades earlier had overtaken Elba as the largest municipality in Coffee County. The second county courthouse added in Enterprise was a hard pill to swallow for some Elba old-timers. To add insult to injury, Enterprise was getting more attention as a football program, too, if for no other reason it played in a much larger classification.

It was an October night in Elba, against Enterprise, when it happened on just the second play of the game. The Tigers, running the veer formation, handed off to their bread and butter. Future Troy State Trojan Sherman Wilkinson had a bead on Johnny, and Wilkinson hit him. He hit him real hard. So hard in fact, Johnny pulled himself off the ground and promptly walked to the Enterprise huddle. His teammates recognized what was going on and grabbed Johnny, and rather than signaling to the sidelines, they walked a woozy Johnny back to the Tigers' huddle.

Elba coaches sent a player to replace Johnny, but he would send another player out. They tried it again and Johnny repeated his previous act. He wasn't going to leave the game, certainly not against Enterprise.

It was the 1970s and the dangers of concussions were hardly on anyone's radar. If you were knocked "silly," you "got your bell rung." You were expected to shake it off and get back to the task at hand.

The only reason Johnny knows even today that he was hit hard enough to "see stars" was his teammates telling him about it the next day, and the picture in the next day's newspaper showed him looking off into nowhere in particular. Despite the collision, Johnny played the entire game. Ironically, on film it may have been his career-best game on defense.

"We played Enterprise really close (losing 20-7), but I don't remember a thing," he said. "I still don't know anything about it. The only thing I knew about was a newspaper clipping and watching the film."

During the game film review the following week, first-year Elba Coach Mac Champion said, 'Johnny, if we can just get you to play defense like that every game.'

As a senior at Elba, Johnny was voted team captain and most valuable player.

If Johnny had an addiction at 18, it was football. He wanted to play more than anything. He'd drink a beer on occasion, but he was so focused on the game that he usually saved the 12-ounce beverages for the off-season. He and three or four friends would often camp out, sometimes on the Pea River and sometimes in a field. They'd sit around and be teenage boys, Johnny recalled, drinking beer or wine coolers, whatever they had managed to get.

"I'm sure it may have had some effect on me, but during football season, I wasn't drinking hardly at all. That was more of a summer thing," he said.

The Tigers finished with a winning season in 1976, but just barely at 6-4. Johnny's senior season at Elba saw a repeat performance at 6-4 under yet another first-year head coach, Mack Wood.

It was a different time. Injuries were handled altogether differently than today. During his senior season, Johnny remembers teammate Don Bradshaw, one of his hunting and fishing friends, suffering what was assumed a leg injury.

"Don came to the sidelines and coaches and managers rubbed his legs as if he had cramps," Johnny said. Bradshaw was sent back in the game, but it was later discovered he had broken a bone in his leg. He was loaded in the ambulance, but en route to the hospital in Enterprise, the ambulance was involved in another wreck.

Bradshaw was country tough, according to Johnny, who recalled his friend and teammate "had toughed it out and returned in time for some late-season action on the field." During the week of practice heading into the final game against Andalusia, Elba coaches were intense. Practices were heated. Toward the end of practice, the coaches led players to the goal line where they would pit the best against the best to see who would come out on top.

Johnny recalled the coaches being particularly on edge while working short-yardage situations. A center broke his face mask and Coach Wood yelled for Bradshaw. Thinking he was finally going to see some action again, Bradshaw sprinted to the huddle, where Wood promptly eased the tension with everyone by asking Bradshaw, being a "farm boy," according to Johnny if he had any hay wire to fix the face mask.

"Coach Wood was probably the most personal of all the coaches I had at Elba," Johnny said. "Of course, I liked him because I was his go-to guy."

Wood had a rule that during the season players were not to go to a swimming pool. The day before fall practice began, just hours shy of Wood's rule being official for the Tigers, Johnny and a few others went to the swimming pool at the town's country club. They were playing a baseball-like game with a tennis ball.

"We were all having a big time," Johnny said. There were only two bases, home and first. First base was on a corner of the pool. If a player played off too far he could get picked off. That's precisely what someone tried to do to Johnny, and when he ducked to avoid the tennis ball, he hit his head on a concrete corner of the pool. His coaches were not pleased when he showed up on the first day of practice with a sore head.

Johnny would graduate spring 1978. He had played for five Tiger head coaches in four seasons. "I really think playing for a different coach each year prepared me to go to Alabama," he said. "I had to earn my spot each time there was a new coach. There was no entitlement."

Johnny would draw the interests of some college coaches, but it wasn't like they were hounding Elba coaches and his parents at each game, and those that did pay attention to him were, for the most part, not big schools.

"I knew I was going to Alabama no matter what," he said. "The little kicker in there for that was up until that time colleges could sign all they wanted. There was no scholarship limit. My senior year in high school was the first time they put a limit that you could only sign 33 people. I knew then they had not been recruiting me really hard.

"I'd talked to some coaches in Tuscaloosa. Florida State had recruited me a little bit, and there was Davidson in North Carolina. Troy really wanted me to walk on. Other than those, there wasn't much. And Florida State wasn't what they are now. Bobby Bowden had only been there just one year or so. They stopped showing a lot of interest because I think they'd gotten the word that I was going to Alabama if I wanted to go due to my parents being prepared to send me there."

Could there be a better marriage?

Bryant had been quoted: "My favorite play is the one where at the end an Alabama player passes the ball back to the official in the end zone." Johnny hoped to one day please Bryant in similar fashion.

Johnny would walk on at Alabama to play for his beloved Crimson

Tide. Heading to Tuscaloosa to play for Bryant and Bama, the last thing Johnny or anyone else worried about was his stability.

Life was good… and it was about to get better.

Marlin "Scooter" Dyess Career at Elba
1953 (8-2 record)

vs. Brantley	won 26-6
vs. Andalusia	won 13-0
vs. Luverne	won 28-0
at Opp	lost 26-0
at Enterprise	won 26-0
vs. Florala	lost 6-0
at Geneva County	won 18-12
at Samson	won 27-6
vs. Geneva	won 34-0
at Charles Henderson	won 40-19

1954 (10-0 record)

(Tigers outscored opponents 338-45)

(Pearino Gaithers first season as Tigers' head coach)

(Marlin Dyess and Thomas Prescott were first-team all-state selections. Bowdoin, Brown, Folson, Roland Powell, and Mack Wise were honorable mention all-state)

(Tigers shutout 7 of 10 opponents, including first 6 of season)

(Final game at Dothan was not originally scheduled but decided on late in season)

at Brantley	won 33-0
at Luverne	won 27-0
vs. Opp	won 27-0
vs. Enterprise	won 48-0
at Florala	won 33-0

vs. Geneva County	won 49-0
vs. Samson	won 33-19
at Andalusia	won 34-19
vs. Charles Henderson	won 41-7
at Dothan	won 13-0

1955 (10-0 record)

(Tigers outscored opponents 344-37)

(Marlin Dyess and Mack Wise were each first-team all-state selections. Charles Clark and Burkett were honorable mention all-state.)

(Elba capped off a 24-game winning streak)

vs. Luverne	won 47-0
at Opp	won 13-6
at Enterprise	won 21-12
vs. Florala	won 34-0
at Geneva County	won 33-6
at Samson	won 34-7
vs. Geneva	won 24-6
vs. Andalusia	won 33-0
at Charles Henderson	won 45-0
at Ashford	won 60-0

Johnny Dyess Career at Elba
1974 (4-6 record)

The Tigers were 1-4 at home, but 4-1 on the road this season under Paul Bass

at Geneva	lost 25-0
at Luverne	won 13-0
vs. Opp	lost 19-0
at Dale County	won 26-9
at W.S. Neal	lost 28-7
vs. Enterprise	lost 54-7

vs. Greenville won	12-6
vs. Eufaula	lost 40-7
vs. Andalusia	lost 34-7
at Charles Henderson	won 21-18

1975 (5-5 record)

Tigers had two different head coaches during season – Paul Bass and Hinton Johns.

vs. Florala	lost 13-12
vs. Geneva	lost 7-0
vs. Luverne	won 33-19
at Opp	lost 26-7
vs. Dale County	won 26-6
vs. Pike County	won 19-6
at Greenville	won 20-0
at Eufaula	lost 8-6
at Andalusia	lost 40-6
vs. Charles Henderson	won 28-27

1976 (6-4 record)

(finished region runner-up under first-year head coach Mac Champion)

at Pike County	won 22-0
at Geneva	lost 17-0
at Luverne	won 14-13
vs. Opp	won 20-0
at Dale County	won 26-13
vs. Enterprise	lost 20-7
at Charles Henderson	won 28-14
vs. Ashford	won 24-21
vs. Eufaula	lost 20-7
vs. Andalusia	lost 24-14

1977 (6-4 record)

(Mack Wood's first season as head coach at Elba)
(both Dyess and Russ Wood were all-state selections for the Tigers)

vs. Pike County	won 21-18
vs. Geneva	won 32-7
at Luverne	won 35-19
at Opp	lost 25-0
vs. Dale County	won 21-0
at Enterprise	lost 25-7
vs. Charles Henderson	won 20-14
at Ashford	won 34-27
at Eufaula	lost 19-0
vs. Andalusia	lost 28-9

Chapter 6

ANOTHER DYESS

Dyess family photo
The 1954 Elba High School team went undefeated and beat the
much-larger Dothan Tigers in the season-finale Peanut Bowl.

Dyess family photo
Alabama greats Marlin "Scooter" Dyess and Johnny Musso were
honored at halftime of this Crimson Tide game in 2012.

IN 1954, ELBA High School had the Dyess & Wise show – Marlin Dyess and Mack Wise. A half century later, another Dyess lost track of anything wise.

As a high school sophomore, Marlin Dyess had helped his Tigers win their final four games to cap an 8-2 season. Dyess was the Tigers' quarterback, although he admits he was out of position because he was so small he could hardly see over the crouched linemen.

Buddy Nesbitt was recruiting the Wiregrass Area for J.B. "Ears" Whitworth and the University of Alabama at the time, and after watching a couple of practices as well as several Elba games, Nesbitt had a suggestion for the Elba coaches.

"Nesbitt told my high school coach, 'If you'll get him out from under center, I think you'll be amazed at what he can do with a football,'" Marlin Dyess recalled.

As Dyess tradition would later prove, Marlin also had to endure a coaching change as Frank Buckner departed Elba prior to the 1954 season.

It wasn't as if Marlin Dyess had been an imposing figure at a somewhat miniscule 5-foot, 6-inches and 150 pounds.

As a high school junior, Dyess was switched to running back as well as playing a bit at receiver. Implementing a two-halfback set – Wise at right halfback and Dyess at left halfback. Wise weighed about 170 pounds.

Pearine Gaithers would coach Elba for Marlin's final two years, going a perfect 10-0 each season. He split after two seasons with the incredible pre-playoff record of 20-0.

There was, however, something of a makeshift playoff game Marlin's junior season. Elba had steamrolled its first six opponents, shutting out all six. The Tigers gave up 45 points in the next three games, but were still unbeaten at 9-0.

Mighty Dothan, the much-larger town in the southeast corner of Alabama, was 7-2, losing only 6-2 at St. Benedictine, Florida, and 27-13 to Mobile's Murphy High. Dothan didn't want to hear all the talk about how Elba, 45 miles away, had the best football team in the Wiregrass Area, so a season-finale was set for Dothan's home field.

The game would be called the Peanut Bowl, paying homage to the town's large agricultural crop. Elba got nearby Geneva High School to agree to cancel its scheduled game for the season-finale. The Peanut Bowl was set for Thanksgiving Day, Nov. 25, 1954.

Between the two programs, there had been 10 shutouts in the combined first 18 games. It became 11 after their meeting as Elba knocked off Dothan 13-0 before a stunned crowd of mostly Dothan fans.

"We did have a good football team, an unusually good team," Dyess said. "We had a bunch of guys that came together. We had good linemen and good backs. I have buddies from Lanier High in Montgomery and they lost to Dothan that year, so I always tell them that Elba was better than Lanier that year."

Dothan player and future longtime college coach Bud Casey, who coached Bo Jackson while at Auburn, recalled once before his passing that the 1954 Elba squad was the best football team he'd ever seen. Casey was later a teammate of Marlin Dyess at Alabama.

"You hear a lot about Marlin Dyess and Mack Wise from that era of Elba football, but Elba had 11 players on the field who could all play well," Casey said. "We played them in the Peanut Bowl at the end of the 1954 season and they whipped us all over the field the whole game. That Elba team was the best one I ever saw."

In fact, seven Elba players from the 1954 squad were selected to all-state teams.

Mack Wise made up the other half of the Dyess & Wise Show. "I guess we just had more 'want to' over there at Elba," Wise said. "If we didn't have somebody at least down 12 or 14 points in the first quarter, something was wrong."

Marlin's senior season at Elba, Gaither's Tigers were even stingier, allowing a mere 37 points. Only once did a team score twice on Elba and that was in a 21-12 Tigers' win at Enterprise.

Georgia Tech was playing smaller running backs during that era and wanted Dyess. He had been valedictorian of his class, so getting him admitted at any university would not be an issue.

On the day he would sign with Alabama, the Elba High School principal called Dyess into his office and said there was a scholarship sent to him from Georgia Tech.

"I almost went to Georgia Tech," Dyess said. "I went to Tech several times on recruiting trips. But my mind was already made up. I wanted to go to Alabama. I didn't have any reason because nobody in my family had ever gone there before.

"I was small, but I wanted to play football at Alabama as bad as anybody could ever want to. But, you know, a fast 200-pounder is better than a fast 150-pounder any way you look at it. I had two great years and I got to play in the high school all-star game. I had real good stats. I had all the credentials to go on to school and I had some teachers that really helped me, writing resumes and other things."

The Dyess & Wise Show continued after Elba, as they took their talents to Alabama, where they played for new Crimson Tide coach Paul "Bear" Bryant. Calcium deposits in Wise's ankle forced him to leave the game following his sophomore season at Alabama.

Dyess admitted he was homesick, even lonesome in Tuscaloosa, a country boy hours away from the farm he'd grown up on in Elba.

"A lot of the other players were too," he said. "But always in my mind I never wanted to quit… and we had a ton of people quit."

In 1958, Bryant's first season as head coach of the Tide, Alabama won more games (five) than the previous three seasons under Jennings "Ears" Whitworth.

"Coach Whitworth was a fine person," Dyess said. "He was a real good guy. But, nobody was afraid of him. You were afraid of Coach Bryant, and the assistant coaches were too. He could be mean as a snake. He was only 45 when he came there. He got down there with the linemen and he participated in stuff."

Bryant took the players leftover from Whitworth's disasterous three seasons at Alabama. Whitworth had, in succession, managed to go 0-10, followed by back-to-back 2-7-1 campaigns. Dyess recalled the team taking a straw poll after the firing of Whitworth. Word had already spread of Bryant's rugged reputation. No one, Dyess included, voted for Bryant. Nevertheless, "Ears" was out. "Bear" was in. Only eight seniors-to-be with the Crimson Tide stayed for their final season.

"Nobody wanted Bryant because we'd heard all the stories," Dyess said. "Then, after Coach (Gene) Stallings became friends with all of us and he'd gone through all that Junction (Texas) stuff (when Bryant was at Texas A&M), he said we went through the same things when Coach Bryant came to Alabama that they went through at Texas A&M, but the only difference is they did it and lived in Quonset huts in all of that Texas heat and we lived in a dorm. We didn't have air conditioning, but we did live in a dorm, which made it easier to rest. Coach Bryant did put air conditioning our place the second or third year he was there."

Prior to his junior season in 1959 at Alabama, Dyess watched as 30 players left the team, some in the spring and some during fall practices, as Bryant's toughness set a foundation for the future. It was not unlike what had taken place under Bryant's leadership at Texas A&M with the now famous Junction Boys situation. Dyess said many of the players that left the Alabama squad were better football players than those that stayed. In fact, of the 80-plus players that Dyess dressed out with on the freshman squad, only three remained by the time he was a senior. "Coach Bryant cleaned out most of them," Dyess said.

Dyess said many players were scared of Bryant before they even met him. Many players left the Alabama program after Bryant began putting them through a spring practice like they'd never experienced.

Marlin Dyess, like other Alabama players, had received word Bryant wanted to meet with each player before spring practice.

"The first time I ever met (Bryant) was between classes," Dyess said. "I had a break in classes and went over there and I was hoping he'd be in the hallway. Sure enough, he was. I was going down to meet him and he didn't even acknowledge that I was around. You wouldn't have even known I was in the hallway. We'd never met. He'd just come on campus in January. I thought, well, I better brave up and say something, so I did. I said, 'Coach, you want to talk to each one of the players individually. I thought I'd come over and meet with you.'"

Bryant glared at the smallish Marlin Dyess and snapped, "Who the hell are you, the water boy?" Dyess wanted to hide, but introduced himself, anyway.

Bryant would give Marlin the nickname "Scooter" after Dyess returned a punt again against Tulane in New Orleans. When he came off the field, Bryant slapped Marlin on his rear end and said, "That's how you do it, 'Scooter.'" It was the first time Marlin said he'd ever been called "Scooter," but it stuck with his teammates, and eventually the student body. Today, he must tell people that Marlin and 'Scooter' are one in the same. "I went by Marlin for 20 years then got stuck with 'Scooter,'" he laughed.

Players were gun shy of Bryant, particularly after going through his rigorous practices.

On one occasion, Marlin Dyess was walking from his down room to practice. He didn't have a vehicle while attending college. A car pulled up alongside him. It was Bryant.

"'Scooter,' you want a ride?" Bryant asked.

The Post Office was off to the right. "I had to think real quick," Dyess said. "I said, 'Coach, I appreciate it but I'm going over here to get my mail.' That wasn't where I was headed, but it was after he asked me that. I didn't want to ride in that car with him. You felt like you were in there with the warden or something."

As a junior – the same year his nephew, Johnny, was born – "Scooter" Dyess helped the Tide beat rival Auburn, ranked 11th nationally, for the first time in five seasons. He scored the game's only touchdown at Birmingham's Legion Field in a 10-0 victory on his only TD reception of the season. He only scored two touchdowns all year. He was elected captain of the team for seven games and as a permanent captain by his teammates.

"Scooter" scored seven touchdowns during his career with the Crimson Tide, four on receptions and three on the ground. He was selected to the Senior Bowl and the Blue-Gray Classic as well as getting to play in the Liberty Bowl.

Six seasons after Whitworth's Tide was winless, Bryant won a national championship at his alma mater in 1961. "Scooter" Dyess said with pride that Bryant had labeled his first Alabama team, "The Turnaround Team" in Tuscaloosa. Bryant would eventually win six national titles as head coach of the Crimson Tide.

Today, "Scooter" Dyess remembers Bryant as a "great man."

During his senior season, Dyess, prior to a trip to play Penn State in the Liberty Bowl, learned he was named as a permanent captain. Such captains were chosen for their performance and efforts during the season.

"When we came out of the meeting – I won't ever forget it because he rarely warmed up to you – we were going out the door and he put his hand on my shoulder and he said, ''Scooter,' I think they made a great choice today.' I said, 'Thank you, Coach.' So I thought boy, I've gone from water boy to the captain.

"Coach Bryant came in and that was like turning dark into light. He was really good to me. I loved Coach Bryant, I really did."

At one point, "Scooter" Dyess worked for Larry Striplin's Disco Aluminum in Selma, the same business that had lured former Tide player, Tennessee coach and future Alabama Athletic Director Bill Battle, to work after his coaching career.

"Scooter" Dyess now lives in Montgomery, the capital city of Alabama, where he built a successful business before retiring. He is a deacon at his church. In 2012, he was honored alongside Alabama's legendary running back Johnny Musso at halftime of a game. They each received the Paul W. Bryant Alumni-Athlete Award, one presented to former Crimson Tide players based on their character, contributions to society, professional achievement and service. Past recipients of the award include Bart Starr, Ozzie Newsome, Dwight Stephenson, Lee Roy Jordan, Harry Gilmer, Bill Battle, Mal Moore, and Cecil "Hootie" Ingram.

For 16 years, "Scooter" Dyess was on the board of directors for the Alabama Sports Hall of Fame.

When Stallings took over as head coach at Alabama in the earlier 1990's, he had "Scooter" Dyess speak to his team, telling them of how to do things and how not to do other things. Alabama won the 1992 national championship.

Musso had been Johnny Dyess' idol as a youngster. Called the "Italian Stallion," Musso was known for both his toughness and breakaway ability. Johnny had emulated Musso many times while playing football in the backyard.

"It was pretty neat them getting that on the same day," Johnny said. "I can remember my Mama and Daddy taking me to go see Alabama play when Musso played. I had a cousin, Johnny Sharpless, that played on that '73 national championship team. He played behind Wayne Wheeler at wide receiver. That was neat and all, but I was Johnny Musso most of the time in my backyard."

"Scooter's" daughter and Johnny's cousin, Lori Ann, would express her desire to attend Auburn, something her father wanted no part of… but he soon realized between his wife and his daughter, he was fighting a losing battle. His wife, Lala Ann, said to "Scooter," 'You went where you wanted to go, so you let her go where she wants to go.'

"Right after I wrote the (tuition) check to Auburn, I had a heart attack," 'Scooter' said. "I don't know if they were connected, but it was ironic. When I was recovering, my dear friend Charlie Stakely said, 'Scooter, I can tell you something worse than a heart attack. You might wind up with an Auburn son-in-law.' So, I started praying right then for an Alabama son-in-law, and wound up with a good one in Keith Shamblin."

Dyess' doctor told the highly motived "Scooter" he needed to slow down, so after leaving his sporting goods business and career in engineering, Dyess formed a brokerage firm.

"Scooter" attended an Iron Bowl once at Auburn, and with the chilly weather that day, he was forced to purchase an Auburn sweatshirt to battle the elements. After telling his daughter he'd rather freeze to death than to wear something with the word 'Auburn' on it, he chose the sweater and promptly turned it inside out.

Chapter 7

BAMA FLIER

Dyess family photo

The only ring Johnny Dyess wears today is the one commemorating
"Bear" Bryant's milestone 315th victory, which came against
archrival Auburn in 1981.

PERCY AND CLARA Ann Dyess wanted Johnny to go wherever he would be happy at college. That was simple. They knew he wanted to go to Alabama. Always had.

"I was blessed," Johnny said. "They had saved and put away for me to go there. Going to college was a given. Football… now that was all on me."

Johnny was hooked on Alabama football from such a young age he can't even remember.

He does, however, recall his first Alabama game. It was 1971 in Tuscaloosa, homecoming, against Virginia Tech. The Crimson Tide rolled to a 35-0 victory, but Johnny was still disappointed. He had followed Bama closely, or as closely as one could from Elba, long before almost every game was televised. His favorite player without question was Alabama running back Johnny "The Italian Stallion" Musso. However, Musso sat out the Virginia Tech game with "turf toe." The Dyess family only made the trek to an Alabama game about once per season, and with Musso a senior, young Johnny would not get a chance to see his idol play again, in person, sporting the No. 22 crimson jersey.

The next season, the Dyess family again went to Tuscaloosa. Johnny was now engrained in Alabama football. There was a driving rainstorm that day, but Johnny made his father, Percy, sit with him to the very last snap, while his mother, Clara Ann, stayed dry in the car with their youngest son, Tim.

"I was hooked," Johnny said, "but, I was hooked before I ever went to a game."

As a freshman at Alabama, Johnny would ride back-and-forth from Elba to Tuscaloosa, the university town nestled an hour from the Mississippi border in West Alabama and more than three hours away from his home. His riding companion was another first-year member of the Tide, Denny Merit of Andalusia. They would trade turns behind the wheel depending on whose car they took.

Merit would leave Alabama, but Elba's Russ Wood would join Bama's football team a year later, so Johnny's ride never ceased. Wood is the son of former Elba Coach Mack Wood. Russ Wood would become a starter for the Tide. Don Horstead, of Elba, later joined Alabama when Johnny was a senior, so traveling to and from home was never an issue.

As a walk-on, Johnny said he had to work especially hard to be a part of the Alabama football team. "You made the team as long as long as you kept coming back and they didn't tell you not to come back," he said. "If you got equipment – a basket with stuff in it – you knew you were still part of the team."

Being a part of the Crimson Tide had indeed been a dream-come-true, and while Johnny was with the team in Bryant's twilight years, that also meant that every game would carry historic significance.

"What made being on the field at Alabama so great was Coach Bryant being out there," Johnny said. "It was more about us pleasing him. We worked for his satisfaction. Of course, he was never satisfied. We didn't want to make him unhappy. I was more of just in awe of him. He was bigger than life."

As a young child, Johnny recalled watching the 1965 Orange Bowl. An undefeated Alabama team from the 1964 regular season had already been declared national champion by the Associated Press, but Joe Namath's fourth-down quarterback sneak in the Orange Bowl was controversially called short of the goal line by officials and Texas won 21-17. "I remember lying on my aunt's floor watching the Orange Bowl and they didn't give Namath credit for scoring... and he did," Johnny said, still upset by the call today. "I cried like a baby."

When Johnny was a freshman, Alabama won its first two contests, against Nebraska and Missouri, but lost its third game – Sept. 23, 1978 – to Southern Cal at Birmingham's Legion Field. The players always read on a locker room blackboard their instructions for when to show up at the football complex to go over film review on Sunday. Usually, that took place in the afternoon, maybe even early evening. Not this time. "We saw it said we were to meet at 7 a.m. on Sunday," Johnny said. "We asked an assistant, 'What about church?' He said,

'Well, I talked to Coach Bryant about that and he said he called the church and most of them have services all day Sunday, even at night. He said we should be finished in time to go for the night service.'"

Bryant had the Crimson Tide players practicing hard. Actually, scout team players like Johnny took the brunt of the physical activity as Bryant and his assistants used them as teaching tools for the starters.

"I told Johnny that walking on was one of the hardest things in the world to do," "Scooter" Dyess said. "I had some good friends up there that walked on when I was playing, but golly bum, you just practice and practice and you're dummies and do everything in the world. I told Johnny that I didn't know if I could've handled that walk-on business. I've seen too many of them get hurt."

Lesson learned. Alabama would win 28 consecutive games and back-to-back national championships in the '78 and '79 seasons. The Tide did not lose again until Nov. 1, 1980, and even then, Alabama was driving for what would have been the go-ahead touchdown late in a 6-3 loss to Mississippi State in Jackson, Mississippi.

"We were prepared," Johnny said. "Coach Bryant made sure of that. We were well prepared."

Johnny, as a freshman, was part of Alabama's 11-1 season that culminated with the memorable 14-7 Sugar Bowl victory over Penn State and in turn a national championship. When he was a sophomore, the Tide went a perfect 12-0, whipped Arkansas in the Sugar Bowl, and won another national championship.

When Johnny was a junior, Bama was 10-2 and crushed Baylor in the Cotton Bowl. Finally, as a senior, Johnny played on Bryant's next-to-last team that went 9-2-1, losing 14-12 to Texas in the Cotton Bowl.

Dyess' senior season – 1981 – at Alabama was filled with historic moments.

The Tide opened the season at LSU's Death Valley. As Bryant entered the stadium his final time, he walked over to the caged LSU mascot, Mike, a live Tiger. Bryant kicked the cage enough to wake up the Tiger, riling up both the large feline as well as early-arriving

LSU fans in Baton Rouge. Johnny believes it was Bryant's way of motivating his players. It must have worked as Alabama cruised to a 24-7 victory.

Johnny would carry the ball only four times all season, but they were in classic matchups in historic venues and in rather close contests. He carried the ball against Tennessee in the famous "Third Saturday in October" meeting at Legion Field, a 38-19 win on Oct. 17. Future Hall of Famer Reggie White led the Volunteers that afternoon in Birmingham.

The Tide had lost by a field goal to Georgia Tech and later tied Southern Miss, meaning if Bryant were going to take the all-time Division I lead in wins over Amos Alonzo Stagg before a bowl game that season, Alabama would have to win out. The Tide beat Tennessee, Rutgers and Mississippi State, then had to travel to Penn State before ending the regular season against arch-rival Auburn.

The Alabama team plane would land at the Harrisburg, Pennsylvania, Airport, near Three-Mile Island, site of the worst nuclear meltdown in U.S. history just two years earlier. The Tide once again used a goal-line stand against the Nittany Lions, and did so by holding Penn State on four consecutive running plays from the one, then held on for a 31-16 victory on Nov. 14, 1981. Even with star running back Curt Warner, Penn State still "shoulda passed," as Marty Lyons had suggested in the classic Sugar Bowl showdown three seasons earlier. The win tied Bryant with Stagg for 314 career victories.

That set up the Iron Bowl, the annual clash between Alabama and Auburn, still being played at a neutral site – Birmingham's Legion Field – at the time. The teams had a week off before the showdown on Nov. 28, something that only added to the pressure on Alabama players, Johnny said, to get the 68-year-old Bryant the record.

Auburn was led by first-year head coach Pat Dye, an assistant under Bryant at Alabama from 1965-73.

Auburn held a 17-14 lead with just 12:58 remaining, before Tide quarterback Walter Lewis led a pair of drives to pull Alabama through for a 28-17 victory. Bryant had the record and Alabama had its ninth consecutive win in the Iron Bowl.

Bryant was carried off the field as the all-time winning coach in Division I history.

Elba's Russ Wood started in the "315" game for Alabama.

Alabama players earned several rings the four years Johnny played for the Tide, but the lone ring Johnny wears today is the one commemorating Bryant's 315 victory.

"It just means more to me," said Johnny, who played mainly on special teams and in mop-up duty late in games. "Winning that 315th game for 'Bear,' that was neat. All of the seniors were captains for that game. Being a senior captain and knowing what it meant was special."

Johnny's years at Alabama were filled with additional milestones. The 1979 game vs. Miami was the first televised game at Tuscaloosa's Bryant-Denny Stadium.

"I told Johnny, just the idea of not quitting, that's the main thing," "Scooter" Dyess said. "You start out something, you complete it."

Johnny's main on-field action came as part of a unit known as the Bama Fliers, Bryant's kickoff return team that was comprised of running backs and defensive backs.

For the most part, Johnny's role was to play running back during practice against a defense that was ranked best in the nation for two-and-a-half of his four seasons there, and was among the best the rest of the time.

"My role was to get the Alabama defense better from the time I graduated high school to the time I accepted my role there," he said. "In turn, it really paid off for me working so hard. Every day I worked against the first-team defense."

Dyess said he was in awe of players he saw each day, having watched them on television and as a fan in the stands the last couple of seasons. "It was a list of who's who," he said. But the awe would get knocked out of him quickly during practice, if not by the list of star defenders, then by the drill sergeants who doubled as assistant coaches for Bryant.

There were calm times with Bryant. Usually, Johnny said, those came during brief moments as they walked out of the tunnel onto the practice field. "Coach Bryant would ask me about "Scooter" all the time," Johnny recalled. "He'd put his arm around you and wanted to know how your mom and dad were doing, and "Scooter." I was so in awe of the man."

Johnny's grandmother didn't understand how the walk-on system worked, and never could grasp why Johnny often wore different numbers on his jersey each season.

Johnny smiled at the memory of his grandmother and said, "I got whatever number they gave me."

As a member on some of Bryant's most legendary teams, nothing was ever – he repeated with emphasis – "never easy." Walk-ons caught the brunt of negative comments following screw-ups by scholarship players.

When the Tide had a particularly bad Saturday performance, walk-ons were expected to be at the field early for a Sunday "let's-get-this-right" practice. The coaches would often take out their frustrations on walk-ons, second-class athletes they figured and a waste of their time except to teach lessons to highly recruited players.

"In Coach Bryant's way of thinking, it was everyone's fault if we lost," Johnny said.

Johnny hated losing as much as anyone to ever don the Alabama jersey, but being a walk-on, he really hated – dreaded – what followed those losses. Bad performances were few and far between, so Johnny believed the thrill of putting on that uniform come Saturday afternoons in the fall made any angry coach's comments directed toward him on other days well worthwhile. "We ran other teams' offense," Johnny said. "Walk-ons were getting it handed to them, I promise you. I was tackled by the best."

Sundays with Bryant following a loss were very rare, but oh were they ever memorable! Having to practice after a loss was Bryant's way of communicating to everybody that they had a job, according to

Johnny. "We got to put on a show on Saturday. Saturday was fun. Practice was not fun. The only thing fun about practice was going in when it ended."

To play for Bryant and his assistants meant keeping it clean in the classroom and certainly in social settings. If you didn't look at your body as your temple, you had better look at it as Bryant's property.

Johnny was living out his dream and there was simply no way he was going to screw this up. Sure, he had a few beers on weekends during the summer, but during football season, even those were taboo. For one, there was no time between classes and practice and weekend games. More importantly, he surely didn't want to catch the wrath of Bryant, or someone such as assistant coach Ken Donahue.

Losing only five times meant for mostly good times in Tuscaloosa during Johnny's four years. Actually, it meant 42 nights celebrating victories. "There would be parties going on all over campus," Johnny said. "But, a lot of the time you'd have family at the game, and you'd want to spend time with them. Or, your girlfriend would be in town. Some fraternities had parties and opened their arms to us. Some weren't so kind. But, we just kind of made our way around."

He admits today that, "Life for Johnny at Alabama was good."

As a high school player at Elba, what few party days he had were during the summer and likely on Saturdays. Friday nights meant games and he was usually too tired to do anything more than spend a little time with his girlfriend. Saturdays usually meant the guys getting together for some R 'n R. That was all just moved a day later once he was playing in college.

A young Johnny had begun playing football in third grade. He discovered rather quickly that he was pretty good, playing the same position, running back, as had his uncle. He also learned about winning. He learned about adapting, playing four years for the Elba High Tigers, each season under the guidance of a different head coach. Ironically, Mack Wood, his final coach at Elba, would remain at the helm of the Tigers for 19 seasons.

Aside from his duties on special teams, the majority of Johnny's in-game action came on the Crimson Tide's junior varsity. Ironically, Alabama did not play a JV football game after a 31-7 victory over Marion Military Institute in 1981, Johnny's senior season, for 21 years.

In a rare football doubleheader, Alabama and Ole Miss played two junior varsity football games on the same day at Bryant-Denny Stadium during Johnny's tenure with the Tide. To qualify for a JV schedule, colleges had to play at least four games and both the Crimson Tide and Rebels needed games; therefore, they played twice. Alabama swept the twin-bill, 13-3 and 3-0.

Alabama's JV team played other SEC JV squads such as Auburn, Ole Miss and Georgia, but also teams such as Marion Military Institute, a junior college, and a team from the Army base at Fort Benning in Columbus, Georgia.

"Fort Benning had some much older guys, including a quarterback (Leamon Hall) who had backed up Roger Staubach earlier with the Dallas Cowboys," Johnny recalled. "Playing Junior varsity probably helped me as much as anything."

The Crimson Tide's JV games were usually played on Thursday or Friday, although the rivalry game with Auburn was played on a Saturday during the varsity's off week prior to the Iron Bowl.

The daily routine for players was grabbing a basket of practice gear from an equipment manager, perhaps with some special instructions for that day, then heading to their lockers and dressing out. There was once when Johnny realized his basket was empty, save for a note that said he was to see Coach Bryant. He had no idea what that meant.

"I sat on his couch," Johnny said of his trip to Bryant's office. "I didn't know if I had been caught doing anything. I was thinking of what I could have done. We were not angels by any means. But then, Coach Bryant said, 'Johnny, we're gonna move you to safety.'"

Alabama's eventual three-time All-SEC and two-time All-American, Tommy Wilcox, had been injured and the Crimson Tide was thin at strong safety.

"I really wasn't big enough, but I played there the rest of the spring practice," Johnny said. "After spring was over Coach Bryant asked me what I was more comfortable with and I thought I was better at blocking than covering."

Wilcox, a native of Hanrahan, Louisiana, became a member of Alabama's All-Century Team and is a member of the Louisiana Sports Hall of Fame. Today, Wilcox stars in his own hunting and fishing show, *Tommy Wilcox Outdoors*.

"There was a lot of hard work that went into playing at Bama," Johnny said. "It was really a dream come true for me. It's what I'd always dreamed of, playing for Alabama and for Coach Bryant."

Johnny seemed much bigger than what the roster noted, checking in at a somewhat small for Southeastern Conference standards at 5-10, 195. He packed on 20 pounds in college only because of the training table and weight room the University provided.

Johnny tried out for the Denver Broncos at Troy State's campus, but his playing days on the gridiron were over after completing his eligibility at Alabama.

Later on, everyone that had played for Bryant from 1971-82 had been invited to Orange Beach, Alabama for a documentary filming of the *Wishbone Boys*. It marked the years Bryant opted for the wishbone offense.

Johnny studied Communications at Alabama, earning his degree in Resource Management from then-Troy State University. Today, he works as his church's custodian. He works at school as a full-time employee. He is the grounds-keeper, assistant football coach and head junior varsity baseball coach.

He will always be a Bama Flier.

Johnny Dyess Career at Alabama

1978 (11-1 record)

(Associated Press National Champions)

vs. Nebraska (at Birmingham)	won 20-3
at Missouri	won 38-20
vs. USC (at Birmingham)	lost 24-14
vs. Vanderbilt	won 51-28
at Washington	won 20-17
vs. Florida	won 23-12
at Tennessee	won 30-17
vs. Virginia Tech	won 35-0
vs. Mississippi State (at Birmingham)	won 35-14
vs. LSU (at Birmingham)	won 31-10
vs. Auburn (at Birmingham)	won 34-16

Sugar Bowl at New Orleans, Louisiana

vs. Penn State	won 14-7

1979 (12-0 record)

AP and Coaches Poll National Champions)

at Georgia Tech	won 30-6
vs. Baylor (at Birmingham)	won 45-0
at Vanderbilt	won 66-3
vs. Wichita State	won 38-0
at Florida	won 40-0
vs. Tennessee (at Birmingham)	won 27-17
vs. Virginia Tech	won 31-7
vs. Mississippi State	won 24-7
at LSU	won 3-0

| vs. Miami | won 30-0 |
| vs. Auburn (at Birmingham) | won 25-18 |

Sugar Bowl at New Orleans, Louisiana

| vs. Arkansas | won 24-9 |

1980 (10-2 record)

vs. Georgia Tech (at Birmingham)	won 26-3
at Ole Miss (at Jackson, Miss.)	won 59-35
vs. Vanderbilt	won 41-0
vs. Kentucky (at Birmingham)	won 45-0
at Rutgers	won 17-13
at Tennessee	won 27-0
vs. Southern Miss	won 42-7
at Mississippi State	lost 6-3
vs. LSU	won 28-7
vs. Notre Dame (at Birmingham)	lost 7-0
vs. Auburn (at Birmingham)	won 34-18

Cotton Bowl at Dallas, Texas

| Vs. Baylor | won 30-2 |

1981 (9-2-1 record)

at LSU	won 24-7
vs. Georgia Tech (at Birmingham)	lost 24-21
at Kentucky	won 19-10
at Vanderbilt	won 28-7
vs. Ole Miss	won 38-7
vs. Southern Miss (at Birmingham)	tied 13-13
vs. Tennessee (at Birmingham)	won 38-19
vs. Rutgers	won 31-7
vs. Mississippi State	won 13-10
at Penn State	won 31-16

vs. Auburn (at Birmingham)	won 28-17

Cotton Bowl at Dallas, Texas

vs. Texas	lost 14-12

Marlin "Scooter" Dyess Career at Alabama

1957 (2-7-1 record)

at LSU	lost 28-0
at Vanderbilt	tied 6-6
at Texas Christian	lost 28-0
vs. Tennessee (at Birmingham)	lost 14-0
vs. Mississippi State	lost 25-13
at Georgia	won 14-13
vs. Tulane (at Mobile) lost 7-0	
vs. Georgia Tech (at Birmingham)	lost 10-7
vs. Mississippi Southern	won 29-2
vs. Auburn (at Birmingham)	lost 40-0

1958 (5-4-1 record)

(Paul "Bear" Bryant's first season as head coach at Alabama)

vs. LSU (at Mobile)	lost 13-3
vs. Vanderbilt (at Birmingham)	tied 0-0
vs. Furman	won 29-6
at Tennessee	lost 14-7
at Mississippi State	won 9-7
vs. Georgia	won 12-0
at Tulane	lost 13-7
at Georgia Tech	won 17-8
vs. Memphis State	won 14-0
vs. Auburn (at Birmingham)	lost 14-8

1959 (7-2-2 record)

at Georgia	lost 17-3
at Houston	won 3-0
at Vanderbilt	tied 7-7
vs. Chattanooga	won 13-0
vs. Tennessee (at Birmingham)	tied 7-7
vs. Mississippi State	won 10-0
vs. Tulane (at Mobile)	won 19-7
vs. Georgia Tech (at Birmingham)	won 9-7
vs. Memphis State	won 14-7
vs. Auburn (at Birmingham)	won 10-0

Liberty Bowl at Philadelphia, Pennsylvania

vs. Penn State	lost 7-0

Chapter 8

HIGH TIDE

Photo courtesy Mike Oakley
Johnny carried the ball twice in the Third Saturday in October
rivalry game with Tennessee at Birmingham's Legion Field in 1981.

JOHNNY'S FORMER ALABAMA teammate, offensive lineman Doug Vickers of Enterprise, also happened to be from Coffee County. While Johnny may not have earned a nickname during his days with the Crimson Tide, he was nevertheless known among his teammates as a big country music fan when it came to locker room tunes.

Vickers said Johnny was always playing music from the then up-and-coming group Alabama. Players would laugh as Johnny would tell anyone that listened, "You watch, they're going to be big one day." He proved prophetic as the band went on to record more than 30 number one hits and sold more than 75 million records, making the group among the top 10 best-selling bands of all time.

To play football under the microscope "Bear" Bryant kept on his football program meant little time for socializing. Between practices, position meetings and going to the training room, Johnny estimates he spent 6 or 7 hours daily on football. That number rose during two-a-day fall practices. He was in classrooms for his regular studies another 5 or 6 hours daily.

"We really didn't have time for a social life," Johnny said. "It was mainly a weekend, off-season type deal. I think all the drinking and drugs really came after football was gone to fill that void.

"No drugs were involved at Alabama. On Friday and Saturday nights, we'd find a spot to drink a beer now and then, but not a lot. We respected Coach Bryant. Back then there was not as much media around, but if he found out something like that, I promise you that there was nothing the media could do that would have been near as bad as what Coach would have done to us."

That said, Johnny admits his priorities were probably not in their proper order during his days with Alabama. "All that time, football and sports were number one for me," he said. "Partying and drinking were number two, family and friends were third, and God was somewhere around fourth or fifth."

Once, Johnny and a teammate went to the dog track in Eutaw owned by Coach Bryant's son, Paul Jr. Another time the two snuck off to Montgomery to see a Molly Hatchet concert. "That was so stupid," Johnny said. "We didn't have social media back then, but the coaches usually found out."

To get through an Alabama practice, players had to be clean. "You couldn't stay out and drink all night," Johnny said. "Hydrating wasn't a big thing back then. They gave us like a little cup of water. It wasn't much better than high school where we drank from a faucet like a dog… and you were glad to get it."

Bryant demanded respect by demanding his players be responsible for their actions. On one night, a player had decided to walk over to a Krystal to get some hamburgers. As he got to the parking lot, he saw a fight in progress and a guy was being beaten up, thoroughly. The player intervened and tried to break up the one-sided fight. The player was stabbed.

The next day, Bryant was not upset at the player for trying to break up the fight, rather that he was out at all at that hour. "As my uncle used to say all the time, nothing good happens after midnight," Johnny said.

When players did head out to clubs, they tried to be incognito. Other men didn't like seeing football players around if there were women, Johnny said. He guesses they were threatened somewhat by the competition. Some of the clubs they went to were rough, but they stayed out of trouble when possible.

"I learned a lot more from that man, Coach Bryant, in the last five or six years than I did while I was at Alabama," Johnny said. "He taught me a lot, but I realize it more today. I know that Bryant had a relationship with God."

Almost all Crimson Tide fans, even those born after Bryant passed away in 1983, hold Bryant in high esteem, but few have the affection as those that learned under him first-hand. The first time Johnny walked onto the field wearing the Alabama jersey, he was elated. But knowing he was representing Bryant made it even more special. He paid the price to do so, but he did it gladly.

"It was just a culmination of a lot of hard work," he said. "It wasn't easy for the first couple of years. When you walked on you were treated different. You're guaranteed nothing. They have no stake in you. I've talked to a lot of people, even in today's world. I talk to so many of these high school kids and they have a dream of playing college football but once they get to a college, and I don't know if coaches mean to do this, and I'm a coach myself now, I want to be fair to every player, but the ones you depend on, the ones that are real players, it's kinda hard not to give them a little more attention, a little more lovin', a little more coachin'. It was certainly that way when I got to college. Those coaches, not only do they have money invested in them because they're paying for their scholarship, but they also have their reputation at stake. You've got Johnny over here who's walking on and you've got Joe over here who've they've recruited and signed. They've staked their reputation in that Joe is one of the best 30 players they can get."

Johnny knows now and even knew then he was not one of those elite players.

Yet, suddenly, Johnny's at mighty Alabama and he's ahead of Joe on the depth chart due to whatever performances took place at practice. "I was ahead of scholarship guys at times," Johnny said. "It kinda makes that coach that recruited Joe look bad. He missed. Why weren't you recruiting Johnny? Maybe it put doubt into Coach Bryant's mind. There were other walk-ons out there that were up in the depth chart at times, too. But, you didn't get that preferential treatment like the recruited guys.

"You got the worst practice jersey, the socks that wouldn't stay up, the jocks that had the band stretched out, the pants didn't fit the best, the shoes were OK… but, you had to prove yourself every day."

It was never abusive treatment, Johnny said, and as time wore on, he showed a work ethic that got him treated a bit better than the season before.

Fans around the Southeastern Conference could be a little tough to deal with considering they all wanted their shot at Alabama, long considered the king of the league.

"The only place we really received a bad reception was at LSU," he recalled, "but when I was a junior (1980) and we were playing at Tennessee, we began walking around the field in walk-thrus and the student section was already packed. When we got in front of them they began unloading on us with oranges. Coach Bryant didn't like that too much. He used that as motivation."

Again, it worked, as Alabama rolled to a 27-0 victory over the Vols.

Tennessee was a very special game each season at Alabama, right up there, Johnny said, with the in-state battle against Auburn in the Iron Bowl. Bryant and many of his staff, particularly head trainer Jim Goosetree, held disdain for the Volunteers. Goosetree handed out cigars to the 1961 Tide after a win during a stretch that had been very lean against their rivals from the north. He wanted a bigger than usual celebration, it has been said. Goosetree was a native of Tennessee, but worked for Alabama throughout Bryant's career there.

Johnny was just a freshman in 1978 when Alabama was preparing to make the trek to Knoxville to meet the Vols. Scout team members got their practice instructions each day from notes on a large board in the dressing room. On this particular Monday, there was a note telling all scout teamers to go to the equipment room. Johnny and others were unsure what this meant, but went there all the same.

"Goosetree hated Tennessee," Johnny said. "He had all of us on the scout team wear orange tape on the back of our helmets with white T's on them. We had to go out to practice that way. After about the third period of practice I was taking that off my helmet. Those guys were killing us."

That motivation worked too, as Alabama won 30-17.

Goosetree was old school and treated players that way. "He (Goosetree) was not pleasant," Johnny said. "He wanted you to stay out of the training room. If you skinned your arms on the Astroturf they would rub it out with alcohol and peroxide. You had to do it because that stuff in the AstroTurf would fester. It hurt bad, but their mentality was that stuff would keep you out of there."

Nothing was easy at Alabama. Defensive line coach Ken Donahue was considered among the toughest in the business. Bryant liked that because he wanted his players tough. Donahue had played at Tennessee under head coach Gen. Bob Neyland. He would later be an assistant for the Vols under Johnny Majors.

Donahue was known for running the "Oklahoma drill," a practice begun by then-OU head coach Bud Wilkinson. The helmet-popping drill was a scary one for the Alabama offense as there were times the three guys lining up on defense were All-Americans.

During Bryant's final years, he once dozed off high up in his famous tower, where he watched practice. No one, Johnny said, would dare wake up the coach on their own. Donahue figured he would move the drill below Bryant's tower and let the sound of players hitting each other wake up the aging coach. It worked.

Johnny still enjoys Crimson Tide football, taking part in alumni activities and even having his photo taken in the chair at the desk of Alabama head coach Nick Saban. The grin is not manufactured. He's like a kid, almost as happy as he was pretending to be Johnny Musso several decades earlier.

It's not as if he has close friends from his days on the Crimson Tide. He just enjoys the pageantry of Game Day. "When you're up there and Bama's playin' you see a few people after the game, but it's such a big crowd and such chaos now," he explained.

Johnny called being in the "A Club" one of his great honors, and says when he is around former Alabama athletes – from all sports – they share a common bond. It makes him feel involved again in Tuscaloosa, or even better, with the traditionally powerful program. "I was never around any of that when I played," Johnny said of the pre-game festivities. "I wasn't around it for a long time after I left. I hardly went to any games for a period of time. I watched them, just never went to the games. I carried my wife up there a time or two. From the time I was 37 to 49 I probably went to just a handful of games. It just wasn't a big priority for me. I kept my tickets though. I would sell them to someone else. It was tough for me to go because I busy doing other stuff… mostly drugs."

One game he should have stayed away from was the second game of the 1992 season at Birmingham's Legion Field. While his beloved Tide would stave off Southern Miss, 17-10, en route to a magical 13-0 season that resulted in the first post-Bryant national championship, it didn't end as well for Johnny.

He had taken a cousin and others to the game. His guests had never attended an Alabama game.

"It was a big party," Johnny said. "After the game, we drank in the parking lot. We decided to go to Baumhower's (restaurant). We left there about 10 (p.m.), drinking the whole time. I knew the area and I was stupid, so I said I'd drive us out to the interstate and when we got there I was going to let my cousin drive. I got to the interstate and decided I was going to go down a couple of exits, then pull over. We weren't even past the first exit when I saw the blue lights."

There was no way to hide the fact Johnny was intoxicated and soon he was hauled off to the Shelby County Jail in Columbiana, about 45 minutes south of Legion Field. Law enforcement had no plans to let Johnny leave anytime soon, so his cousin had to take his Jeep back to Elba. The next morning, the cousin drove Johnny's vehicle to his parents' house and informed them of the previous night's events. Johnny was still locked up, and the cousin rode with Percy and Clara Ann back to bail him out.

"There weren't two words said the entire way back," Johnny said. "It was not good. It was a quiet ride home. We stopped somewhere on the way back to eat and they still weren't talkin.'"

Chapter 9

—⚬—

EARLY TROUBLE

"The Devil made me do it the first time.
The second time I done it on my own." – Billy Joe Shaver

JOHNNY'S TEENAGE YEARS had been that of a typical American youth. When he and some friends could break away, they would drink beer. He does recall experimenting with smoking marijuana during those supposedly formidable years, but all told, he was probably far more decent that the average teen-age boy.

As his high school days progressed, Johnny got in trouble a couple of times for drinking and driving, but those hadn't been considered serious offenses. After all, while such an act was not looked upon kindly, laws in the seventies for drinking and driving were hardly severe. In Elba, Johnny said, drugs were not really "a thing" in those days. Elba and all of Coffee County were dry at the time, meaning the government forbid the sale of alcoholic beverages.

"Drugs weren't prevalent at all," Johnny said. "My beer experimentation started out with a buddy of mine getting one or two out of his granddaddy's garage, and it kind of grew from there."

He would drink more after graduating from high school. During the first year following Johnny's return to Elba from his days in Tuscaloosa, he picked up a DUI charge in Troy, a short 30-mile drive to the northeast. Troy was another college town. While the penalties were far less harsh during 1982 than they are today, his offenses were beginning to pile up. Johnny wound up getting eight or nine of them; he forgets the exact number.

"I had a pattern going," he said. "I always kept my license instead of turning it in. If there was a roadblock and they didn't go back to check my history like they do now, I was good to go, as long of course that I was not drunk. I'd get my license back and lose it again with another DUI. I'd go about every three years, then get another one. I guess I wasn't too concerned. I'd lose my license for a while, but I never stopped driving."

Johnny was stopped more than once driving without a license. But, as would become his routine, he had either his parents or some friends bail him out. He picked up his last two DUIs in the same week, one in Coffee County and the other in adjoining Covington County. He now jokes that he was spreading the wealth around Southeast Alabama.

Johnny did not have a license on the first of the two-in-a-week DUIs, and with new laws in place, he was promptly sentenced to a mandatory 60 days in jail. Up to that point, Johnny said it had always worked out where after five years from a DUI, his count started over. He had bonded out on the Coffee County arrest, but since court kept getting postponed for one reason or another, he had time on his hands. That's when he headed to Covington County. This time, when he was pulled over, Johnny had drugs in his pocket. That meant a felony violation.

The court made a deal with Johnny. All he had to do was plead guilty to the DUI and the drug charges would be dropped. "I thought, 'Yeah!' So, I agreed to that."

Nevertheless, his second DUI got Johnny a trip to the Covington County Jail, which was exceptionally poor timing because he was incarcerated in Opp when his court date finally arrived in Coffee County. They took Johnny from the Covington County Jail to the Coffee County courtroom. Johnny was dressed in his jail-dispensed striped clothes. It was, to say the least, not the desired attire to be facing a different judge… in a different county…. on a separate DUI charge from the one that put him in the stripes in the first place.

This time, Johnny faced a fourth-and-long, very long. He was facing what was supposed to be a mandatory year of incarceration at a state prison because of his compilation of DUI charges.

As would be the case, although Johnny couldn't see it then, he believes now that a higher power had a hand in his fortune. There was remodeling taking place in the courtroom in Elba and the judge there had moved court into a small office downstairs. The arresting officer was in the room, as is necessary. When everyone walked out, including the arresting state trooper and Johnny, the judge recognized Johnny.

The judge was Steven Blair. He told Johnny to step back inside the room. Blair asked the typical, "What are you doing here?" "I told him," Johnny said.

Blair pulled up Johnny's arrest record and proceeded to give it a thorough read. "You know you're supposed to be getting a year state time on this because of the number of convictions, right?" Bair asked… or perhaps it was more of a threat to Johnny.

There sat Johnny and the judge in the little room. Blair wanted to know why and how Johnny had picked up the DUIs. Johnny answered him. Blair sentenced Johnny, allowing him to serve his sentence in Coffee County concurrent with his Covington County sentence.

"I promised Judge Blair that day in court that if he helped me he never would see me before him again as far as drinking and driving," Johnny said. "I'm sure he'd heard it all before. And I didn't quit drinking, but I didn't drink and drive anymore. I gave the vehicle to my Dad… and he sold it."

Chapter 10

RAISED RIGHT

Dyess family photo
Clara Ann and Percy Dyess were both educators and well-respected
members of the community.

GENES ARE AN amazing thing. If science could, perhaps the genes of Johnny's parents would be cloned because they were great ones. Johnny had the genes of his parents, no question. He just lost them for a while.

Johnny's father was a retired educator who had also been born and raised in Elba. Percy Dyess had joined the Air Force and served a short period in France. Upon his return to Coffee County, Percy became a teacher. A brother to Alabama football great Marlin "Scooter" Dyess, Percy earned a degree from Troy State University before getting his Master's in Education from Alabama. Soon, he became the principal at nearby New Brockton. Percy was at New Brockton during integration, and resigned from his post following an incident where he had wanted equal punishment between a white student and an African-American student. He felt he had not received full support from his board, despite doing what he felt was the right thing. The white student was believed to be in higher standing with the board, simply because of the color of his skin, and Percy felt he couldn't work under such conditions. This only cemented his decision to leave.

Things would be OK, the Dyess family figured, as they would make an even bigger effort to make Clara Ann's business, Dyess Quality Fabrics, pay off. They had owned the shop a few years, but Percy had been too busy with his main job to spend much time at the shop. Now, they planned, profits from the shop would get Johnny a car for his senior year of high school.

Percy and Clara Ann would drive back and forth to Atlanta buying fabrics for the business, filling the family station wagon before returning to Elba with the goods. It would be a trip Johnny would later make routinely, only the product he received was far different than fabrics his parents had stuffed into their vehicle.

However, one week after his resignation as New Brockton's principal, Percy Dyess was hired by McArthur State College in Opp in the school's business department.

Percy and Clara Ann kept true to their plan and prior to his senior year of high school, Johnny was given a brand new 1977 Chevy Camaro, red, of course.

Clara Ann had also been born and raised in Elba. She, too, was in education, majoring in Education at Alabama. Ironically, she taught home economics at New Brockton and later at Elba, including having Johnny as a student his senior year.

Johnny was born Nov. 13, 1959, in Elba, and that's precisely where he's made his bed ever since, aside from his four years at the University of Alabama, the year he was married and living in Opp, and the dark nights drugs kept him from his home.

Even growing up in a small town, teenage boys weren't isolated from mischief. Johnny recalled, "On Saturday, you know, in the afternoons, well, people knew, usually, we'd meet up at the Rec Center," he said. "It was a skating rink-type building. They'd open it up on Saturday night for teenagers. That was kind of the gathering point. The people that had cars, we'd leave from there and go to Opp over in Covington County."

Opp, a town only about 17 miles from Elba, was just outside of Coffee County to the west, but Johnny said it may as well have been far, far away. "We had certain stores down there we knew we could go to and buy beer," he said. "It didn't matter that we were all underage. We had developed a relationship with these older men. They were in it for the money. We did it on a regular basis and there were two or three places that would sell it to us. They probably figured that we were gonna get it one way or another, so they might as well sell it to us and make some money. Up until then, we'd just give older guys money to get the beer for us… you know, juniors and seniors. That's how we figured out where to go. Eventually one of us would go with them and eventually they'd say, 'Well, you gotta go in and get your own this time.' Once the ice was broken and they knew you had the money they'd sell it to you. And back then, the beverage control people were a lot more lax than they are now."

In groups of three or four, Johnny and his friends would gather at a store where they knew the guy behind the counter. They'd walk in, grab their beer of choice and hand the man their money.

"He'd take it outside and put it in the trunk of the car for us," Johnny recalled. "We weren't handling it. We never got stopped during that time. The fun thing to do was to buy little pony Millers so you had more bottles to throw at signs. The drinking part of the trip was coming back. A lot of times we'd go somewhere and stop and have a little party. It wasn't like we were drinking a lot of beer. Six or seven beers – 8-ounce ponies – when you're 15 or 16 and don't drink a lot and you've got a pretty good buzz going."

Johnny and his friends would hang out long enough for the buzz to wear off before they went home to unassuming parents, or parents that just didn't want to know. Sometimes, they just had what they called a campout, although he said, looking back, "We thought we were fooling everybody, but after a while I'm sure they caught on."

Johnny remembers being caught after drinking for the first time by his parents. "Yeah, that wasn't good," he said. "But it was one of those, you know, 'You don't need to be doing it.' I was maybe put on restriction for a little while."

As Johnny and his friends got older, becoming juniors and seniors in high school, most of them had their own vehicles. Their plans were more evolved. They'd get the beer in advance, then go hang out with their girls rather than wasting precious time driving to Opp and back. Although, looking back, Johnny felt as if the real fun part of the early beer-drinking days was the drive with his friends to get the beer.

Johnny was hardly a bad guy; his beer drinking was very limited. The girlfriend he was seeing was not into drinking. And there was always football, which required Johnny to remain in shape by working out. "My dream was to play football at Alabama," he said. "That was my goal. That was my number one goal."

He had accomplished his goal, thanks in part by his parents' savings and his own desire.

When drugs entered Johnny's life, he did his best to keep their presence from his parents. When legal troubles began mounting, Johnny said it was simply not spoken of between himself and his parents. When he'd picked up the two DUI's on the same day, there was no way to keep it from them, since he was locked up.

"It was usually just Daddy telling me that I knew better," Johnny said. "There really wasn't anything to explain. I guess they just thought this was the way it was going to be."

After he was out on his own, when Johnny's parents visited his house, hiding meth lab products was the easy part. But there is a smell that goes along with the chemicals involved. A can of Lysol will hardly mask an odor, but the smell of meth is much harder to conceal. He thinks they noticed, although he had been wise to keep the lab outside.

"For one, my parents hardly ever came to my house," Johnny recalled. "I would always go to theirs. When I'd go to work, I'm sure they were in and out over there because I know they found a bunch of stuff one time and threw it all away. We had a long talk. You know, 'It's not good for you. You need to quit.' I'd say, 'I'll quit,' and that lasted just a short little bit."

Johnny is quick to steer any wayward blame from his parents. "None of it is on them," he said. "They did everything they could. If anything, they probably went too far enabling me, which all parents do. I was raised by Christian parents. I have no excuses for any of the stuff I took them through."

Nevertheless, he was digging his parents' grave.

Percy and Clara Ann were devoted to their church, Westside Baptist in Elba. The shame Johnny felt each time he was arrested, particularly the times he couldn't keep from his parents, was mighty. "You just feel like you disappointed them," Johnny said.

When he was locked up for the DUI's, he said, "It wasn't my first time to disappoint them, and it wasn't my first time to be locked up, either. It was like, 'Here we go again.'"

Johnny had skated through most of his teenage years, mostly because he kept the alcohol/drug abuse to a minimum. There were never major instances, but on a couple of occasions, Johnny and some buddies were caught with beer.

Johnny's first brush with the law was, in retrospect, quite juvenile. He and a friend were nabbed by Elba police after drinking too much beer and playing games some restless teenagers play in town late at night. They'd been on Pea River gigging frogs, and later met some others who'd provided the beer. The youngsters were soon, as Johnny recalled, drunk. When the party ended, they drove through town showing off the frogs. They were supposed to be home by midnight, but they were bragging mightily in the parking lot of Big Bear, a local grocery store. They were towing a boat behind the friend's truck, and although Johnny was of legal age to drive at 16, his friend was driving and he was only 15.

Upon leaving, they went from one stop light to the other, seeing just how fast they could get the truck going in short stretches. The friend was betting Johnny how fast he could go. He got to going so fast that he was unable to stop at one stop light, sliding underneath it, in fact. On the other side of the stop light sat a police officer.

"Of course, the police came over and checked us and my friend didn't have a license," Johnny said. "I'm sure it didn't take them but a minute to figure out we'd been drinking."

The two boys were taken to the police station, where the friend's father was called to pick them up. The man, who had to be awakened, told Johnny he was going to call Mr. Dyess. "I said 'No, you don't need to do that. I'll tell him when I go home tomorrow.' So, I thought, well, that'll be the end of that."

The next morning, Johnny went home and stayed around the house all day.

"All day, I ain't told them nothing," he said. "I was thinking I'd skated by again. Then about dark, my buddy's daddy calls my mama and daddy and asks them if I'd told them what happened the night before. Of course, I hadn't. They came out and confronted me. I had to own up that we'd gotten caught by the police."

Later on, after his football playing days were over at Elba and Alabama, Johnny returned with his priorities all out of order. "When I left Alabama, I drank and smoked a lot of pot."

Chapter 11

$\sim\!\!\sim\!\!\sim$

Coming Home

AFTER RETURNING FROM Tuscaloosa to Elba, Johnny had moved back in with his parents, but that had been fine. Johnny began hanging around guys he had always known, but he was never particularly close to them. It was during some of their get-togethers that he was introduced to cocaine by his companions.

While he continued drinking beer and smoking marijuana on occasion, it was cocaine that came into play during his non-work hours with his new friends. Nevertheless, Johnny had begun to seek a high that better fit his lifestyle. Cocaine was not that drug.

Cocaine made him "feel funny," and it didn't leave Johnny high for long. The drug was also an expensive habit, , and Johnny's limited budget was not conducive to having cocaine available regularly.

When it was available, Johnny made sure to only use the drug around certain individuals. Despite his lifestyle, he still tried not to blow his cover with others, perhaps even being embarrassed that he had slipped from the town's once-admired football star to being considered a drug addict.

Still living with his parents, Johnny believes they knew their older son came into the house looking different at times, but they just didn't say much about his appearance.

Another downside of cocaine was its cost. A couple of hundred dollars back then was about half of Johnny's paycheck that literally was going up his nose, and even that amount would only last a couple of days. If it was shared with any friends, then it could be a one-night thing. "The cost versus the high versus the feeling, well, I had enough sense to know that wasn't me," he said. "I still did it every now and then, but it just wasn't me. I just kinda strayed away from it pretty much.

"Cocaine really wasn't my thing. I kinda liked the feeling of it, the way it made you feel. It'd give you a lot of energy, but the downside was that the high didn't last very long. It was one of those things where you just couldn't ever get enough. Thirty minutes later and you wanted more. It's a habit. Your body is just craving it to keep that feeling going, but the downside is just horrible."

Johnny said God had a plan for him even during those early days of hard drug use, but still in his twenties, he still felt the need to run from whatever said plan may be. At this point, he just wanted to run to his next high.

"That's why I tell people that I don't care what they say but marijuana is a gateway drug," Johnny said. "I certainly wouldn't argue with that. I honestly believe it. I think maybe it breaks down your resistance to try something else, and I think alcohol breaks it down for you to try marijuana."

It was April 1985 when Johnny was introduced, at the age of 35, to a drug called Red Rock, an early name for crystal meth. Life was about to change, and the devil, Johnny said, took charge of this life-altering moment in time, he recalled, "I don't think I had ever turned it down, people just knew I wasn't into it." Therefore, it had not been offered to him.

But one night, at a friend's get-together, the drug was presented to him. He accepted.

This time, with this drug, Johnny liked the way it made him

feel and unfortunately, that night was far from his last acceptance of meth.

"I figured this was great," Johnny said. "I wasn't drinking hardly at all. I found myself opening beers and leaving them sitting around full because I didn't care to drink anymore. I just wanted the drug. I figured alcohol had been the cause of my problems because I had eight or nine DUIs, so this was great.

"It's all about choices and I got very good at making bad choices. Meth is a life-controlling drug. It will kill, steal, and destroy everything good in your life."

Among the worst of those poor choices was Red Rock, which had Johnny hooked almost immediately. "I smoked it mainly, but I snorted it a little, too," he said of the new drug. "My first experience was such a high, such a rush. I had a lot of energy, but I couldn't control myself. You become a piddler. I'd start 50 projects, but never finished one. When you're using, most of the time it's with friends, but this was such a selfish drug. You want to save every little bit for yourself. When you run out you gotta go on the hunt. You don't know where you're next (drug) is coming from."

Johnny eventually learned how to manufacture the drug at his residence, and by the time he was making it better than most local cooks, he had settled into a lifestyle that needed little money and even fewer friends to pass the days away.

"I couldn't grow it, so I learned how to make it," he said. "I wasn't interested in selling it. What drove me was how much I could supply for Johnny. If I needed a little money, I could sell a little dope to get more supplies to make even more of the drug. I spent more time perfecting making it than I did studying for any course in college. I wanted it clean."

Johnny said the early drugs, even beer, had been stepping stones to higher highs, and he especially loved the high he was getting from what was now more commonly referred to as "meth."

There was no more football in Johnny's life, aside from watching

Alabama on television or making the occasional trip to see his alma mater in person in Tuscaloosa.

The drug, he recalled, was a bit of a replacement for the good times he'd experienced on the gridiron. "That, and I just had a wild side," he said. "When I was drinking, I got crazy sometimes, but meth was something else."

Chapter 12

———— ∾ ————

FOCUSED ON THE GAME

JOHNNY'S LOVE TO compete was evident the first time he played pick-up football games against his buddies as a young child. Yes, he would play high school football, and later managed four years as a walk-on at Alabama under "Bear" Bryant. Regardless of the size of the crowd, Johnny just wanted to play.

Whatever the sport, or circumstances, Johnny wanted to compete. Never was that more evident than during his first summer (1982) out of football when he wrecked and totaled his prized Camaro en route to a softball game.

The game was at the Enterprise Parks & Recreation fields, about 15 miles from Johnny's home in Elba.

Enterprise has a bypass encircling it. On the northeast side of Boll Weevil Circle, during its construction, Johnny was cruising along to his game. It may not have been football, but it was summer and this was as good way as any to feed his competitive spirit.

Johnny had only glanced down for a moment to change stations on the radio. When he looked up, he saw the cars in front of him had come to a stop as they waited for one in front of them to turn left.

Johnny locked his brakes, but at this point the result was inevitable. It was too late. The Camaro slammed into the back of a man's vehicle, which set off a chain reaction of cars in front of it. Eventually, seven cars were involved in the pileup, although most received only a minor fender-bender of sorts from cars behind them and whatever damage they caused to the car in front of them as they bumped.

The police arrived, but not before Johnny realized his car had suffered the worst damage. In fact, it had met its maker. The entire engine block had been crushed. During the wreck, Johnny's head slammed into the windshield; there was blood to prove it. But, like the hard-nosed football player he'd been, he managed to shake it off. Concussions, he says, were not big concerns in those days. You shook off any injury and moved on. It's what his coaches would have told him, he guessed.

Everyone else had managed to pull their wrecked vehicles to the side of the road. The police officer asked Johnny if he could move his there, too. Johnny obliged by leaning into the driver's side window and putting the car in neutral. He began rolling it, albeit uncontrollably, to the side of Boll Weevil Circle.

Unable to reach the brakes, Johnny saw what was about to happen. It was almost watching it in slow-motion with no way to hit pause. He could not warn the same man he had originally hit as the Camaro once again hit the back of the unlucky fellow's vehicle.

"Sorry," Johnny said, but he had a game to catch, so the apology was quick.

Johnny left the Camaro beside the road, grabbed his softball gear, and hitched a ride to the ball field. Later, a passerby recognized the crumpled car and called Johnny's parents to check on his welfare.

Knowing Johnny had a game, his somewhat frantic parents made a few calls, including eventually the recreation department. In turn, rec department personnel summoned Johnny to a phone. He proceeded to tell them that he was OK, but hey, he was in the middle of a game and he needed to return to his team.

He never did find out what his parents had to pay – or at least their insurance – for the damage he caused that day. Asked if he was on something, he says, "No, but I was probably hung over."

Chapter 13

KLEINERT'S

IN 1967, THE company that would become known a few years later as Kleinert's Inc., agreed to establish a manufacturing plant in Elba, which was actually larger in 1970 – population 4,634 – than in 2010 – population 3,919. Groundbreaking for the 180,000 square-foot facility was held in 1969 for the core manufacturing plant, which developed children's sleepwear and playwear, as well as women's dress shields.

Its founder, I.B. Kleinert, had invented the dress and garment shield category for excessive perspiration in 1869 in New York. Among Isaak Kleinert's inventions shortly around the time of U.S. Presidents Abraham Lincoln, Andrew Johnson and Ulysses S. Grant were the shower cap, shower curtain, baby pant, dress shield, garment shield, sanitary pant and many other products. Kleinert's even supplied the U.S. Army Air Corps rubber life rafts during World War II for pilots forced to ditch planes into the ocean.

Now headquartered in Kutztown, Pennsylvania, Kleinert's added 80,000 square feet to its Elba plant in 1979, and 80,000 more in 1992. Then at 340,000 square feet, Kleinert's Inc. of Alabama was believed to be the most modern plant anywhere in the world for children's apparel.

As Southern as Elba was, Kleinert's sales staff was based in New York City.

At one point, Kleinert's employed about 1,500 people in Elba, and although that was a large percentage of the town's Census, people came from Opp in nearby Covington County and Kinston, New Brockton and Enterprise in Coffee County. The plant supported many Elba families who had few other employment opportunities in their small community.

After Johnny's football days and school work were concluded at Alabama, he returned to his hometown needing to find a real job. Opportunities were hardly growing on vines from which Johnny could pick, at age 22, in Elba, Kleinert's was the obvious place to look, since his grandfather was working as a security guard there. Johnny was good friends with another man working in Kleinert's warehouse, and he was soon hired as a scale operator.

Eventually, a dedicated and hard-working Johnny moved up the ladder, becoming a production planner, and later a buyer and traffic manager. He had joy in his soul and food on the table.

Hearing of an opening for the much-coveted traffic manager's post, Johnny concocted an idea. He had been selected to take Kleinert's executive Victor Mortimier to the Tallahassee, Florida, airport when he left Elba, and figured there would be plenty of time to ask for a favor about the job opening.

Johnny knew Mortimier enjoyed talking and knew Johnny had played for "Bear" Bryant and against Penn State on a couple of memorable occasions.

"The first time I met him, I carried Mr. Victor back to the Dothan (Alabama) airport," Johnny said. "He told me he had a child going to Florida State, which is why he flew into Tallahassee, I guess. He knew I'd played football and he knew my association with Coach Bryant. He was just real intrigued. I think he was maybe a (University of) Pittsburgh guy."

Johnny had become frustrated because, although he had applied for the traffic manager's position, he had yet to hear anything. Days had turned into weeks.

"I was getting to the point where I was going to have to do something else with my life," Johnny said. "I was not wanting to be a scales operator and an hourly employee all of my life. I thought I was qualified for the job and felt I could do it. So, I made up my mind on the way to Tallahassee; when we got within an hour of there, I was going to bring up the question about what was going on with the job."

Johnny and Mortimier had the usual friendly conversation, what was taking place at the company and what was going on in their lives. "We get about an hour away and I ask, 'You know what their plans are about the production planning job opening at the plant?'" Johnny recalled. "It really wasn't his concern. He was over upper-level management. But he said, 'I don't know, have you applied for it?' I said 'Yes sir. I've applied and interviewed. Been two or three weeks and haven't heard anything. He said, 'Well, I'll have to check into that.' I kinda left it at that."

The conversation about the job had been brief, but Mortimier told Johnny to keep his nose clean and continue to work hard. As they reached the airport, Johnny grabbed Victor's luggage to assist him curbside at the terminal. The two shook hands and said their polite "Look forward to seeing you next time" goodbyes. Johnny got back in the car and returned to Elba on this Friday night.

"That Monday, they called me and offered me the job," Johnny said. "I knew then that I'd made some kind of impression on (Mortimier). From then on, me and him, we stayed close."

It was not only a salaried position, but Johnny had his own office. "That was a big step for me personally," he said. "Not having to punch a time clock anymore was a big thing." Johnny would remain at Kleinert's 13 years.

Looking back, Johnny realizes God was trying to help him even then.

Johnny supervised truck drivers, basically orchestrating their routes. The position paid well and meant even more job security for Johnny.

While at Kleinert's, Johnny met a girl, Lisa, from nearby Opp, who would come over with another girl daily to provide food service at the factory. They stocked vending machines, as well as serving breakfast and lunch. The Opp girls would arrive at Kleinert's early, and leave after lunch was served to Kleinert's employees.

"I saw (Lisa) one day and talked to her a little," Johnny recalled. "I asked the girl working with her if Lisa was married and she said, 'No, she's separated.'"

The other girl said Lisa wanted to talk to Johnny. "I said I didn't want to be in the middle of breaking up her family," he said. "I wasn't getting involved in that. I knew I liked her. I could tell she liked me. One day, her friend told me her divorce had been finalized. I got her phone number and called her. We started seeing each other."

Lisa had a child.

Lisa's daughter was only 11-months-old, but that was fine with Johnny, who took to the child immediately, and vice-versa.

Johnny remained active by playing on traveling softball teams. Weekend getaways with the guys opened an avenue Johnny never imagined he'd venture down, but he just shifted into a low gear and moved on, straight to an even darker side of the world of drugs.

Johnny considered himself "pretty clean" while at Kleinert's, at least most of the years he spent there. Marijuana, he said, began creeping more and more into his life while having a few beers with friends on weekends. "It was a beer fest," he said. "The drinking was escalating, but it didn't hurt my job during the week."

However, security was a fleeting thing for Johnny, and soon, his job performance suffered and he frequently came in late for work. Upper management had no choice but to fire Johnny. He had taken his partying to the limit, just as he had taken football as far as it would take him. He tried to keep it to a weekend thing, just like football. He still worked weekdays, but, oh, those weekends.

There was no such thing as drug testing in those days, therefore he never failed one.

"My era was different from Johnny's," "Scooter" Dyess said. "Johnny came up in town. He grew up in a good environment. His mother and daddy were both educators. He had all he needed through high school and everything. That's why I always felt, how did he get off track. It was a good family; he was a good kid. People make mistakes, I know, but he must have got with the wrong crowd and went off in the wrong direction."

Kleinert's has long since left Elba and since 2003 has been incorporated as Hygienics Industries, headquartered in Wayne, Pennsylvania.

Kleinert's had become history, but drugs had Johnny smack dab in the middle of trouble and he was refusing to quit.

Chapter 14

———— ❦ ————

Marriage, Stepdaughter, Divorce

Johnny and Lisa dated almost four years before they split up. Johnny's drinking and marijuana use was not what Lisa had expected and certainly not what she was looking for in a relationship. While she did smoke a few cigarettes on occasion, she was straight-laced when it came to alcohol and drugs.

"Just a country girl from Opp" was how Johnny described Lisa, a girl who had stayed true to her small-town values. While still a good guy, Johnny had lost a large portion of the values Percy and Clara Ann had instilled in him, or those he had received from the town of Elba, or even those he had majored in while studying life and football under "Bear" Bryant at Alabama.

"I never saw her get drunk," Johnny said of Lisa. "If she ever was, I was so drunk I didn't know it."

During their dating, Johnny had become very close to Lisa's daughter, Bridget. Lisa and Johnny would reunite and soon get married… Feb. 2, 1994. Percy and Clara Ann loved Lisa and Bridget and were thrilled their son had married Lisa. They would keep Bridget while Johnny and Lisa went out.

"I had accepted that I loved 'em both," Johnny said of the mother-daughter tandem. "I took (Bridget) like she was my own, and so did my Mother and Daddy." Johnny had taken Lisa to her first Alabama football game during their dating days.

Johnny would start his new life with Lisa and Bridget in Opp as the two purchased a home there. The drive to Kleinert's was relatively short; his promise to clean up his drug and alcohol abuse was not. In fact, things would get worse.

"I slipped around and smoked a little marijuana," Johnny said. "She probably knew I had a little wild side, but I didn't do it around her. We had a good relationship. She didn't really drink or anything, so that kinda slowed things down. I still drank a little bit of beer, like at two or three in afternoon, and that was it. It wasn't a case of getting blasted."

That was coming.

Each morning, Johnny would take his stepdaughter to daycare in Opp, then drive to work in Elba. He'd tell Lisa he was going hunting in the afternoon when he got off work, and in fact he did go to the hunting camp, most often, to meet his buddies. They were less concerned with shooting game than they were drinking and smoking pot. There was also some cocaine use, but it never provided the feeling Johnny was looking for, so beer and pot were his drugs of choice then.

"Lisa begged me and fought with me," Johnny recalled. "It was all on me. I don't see how she put up with it as long as she did. Of course, me partying put our finances in a bind. I wasn't the husband I should have been. It shows the power drugs have because I loved them, Lisa and Bridget. If I have any nightmares in my life today it's letting that relationship slip away. That was a big one. They say it takes two to tango, but I was the one causing everything to be bad. We all want to blame somebody else, but if I had been living my life way I should have, it probably wouldn't have happened."

What had been a problem of smoking marijuana would soon become a much more sinister problem.

At a party, Johnny had been introduced to methamphetamine. It started with a guy Johnny had found employment with after being fired from Kleinert's. The guy lived in a trailer near the even smaller Coffee County town of Kinston. Supposedly, he worked for a company that installed aluminum siding, and he and Johnny did do a little bit of that, but they would do a whole lot more business in the drug world.

Johnny and Lisa's marriage lasted only about two years, because Johnny had stepped up his drug usage. The marriage would end, but his drug habit was just getting its talons into Johnny. When Johnny began working with the guy following his divorce, it became obvious the other man (Johnny doesn't recall his name) was all about consuming drugs and alcohol in ways Johnny never imagined.

Bridget was starting preschool when the divorce occurred. Lisa made it clear she did not want Johnny seeing her daughter. "She did the right thing," Johnny says today. "I understand that now. At the time, I thought it was just cruel." Even today, Johnny smiles as he recalls Bridget referring to him as "Daddy Johnny."

Bridget is now grown, yet still calls Johnny her "Daddy." She calls him on occasion. Johnny returns the favor.

As for Lisa, she and Johnny are now friends. "We're good," Johnny said. Lisa is remarried, but Johnny said he has a good relationship with his former family because God worked it all out for him.

It did not happen overnight.

Chapter 15

UNFORTUNATE MEETING

JOHNNY IS UNSURE today what the guy's name was; he's not even sure if he's still alive. He doubts it. Once the guy was arrested and taken away years ago, Johnny never heard from him again.

Soon after being fired from Kleinert's, Johnny had met the guy who'd share drugs with him at a party; Johnny soon agreed to work with him.

"I was with him a couple of years," Johnny recalled. "We did a little vinyl siding, but not much."

Johnny does remember the guy was known as the "Red Crank Guy." And, he remembers all too well why the guy had such a moniker.

The Red Crank Guy had introduced Johnny to his home-cooked brand of methamphetamine, some of the best Johnny had ever smoked. He tried meth manufactured elsewhere, but it had not compared favorably to the Red Crank Guy's product.

Crank is another name for meth, and red crank refers to a method of cooking the drug that became particularly popular because of its red phosphorus-based ingredient. Regardless, the end product was crystal meth.

There are multiple ways of using the drug: eating, snorting, smoking or injecting it directly into the blood stream with a needle. Johnny's preference was smoking. His new-found partner in crime made quality meth in his trailer house in an isolated part of the county between Elba and Kinston.

Meth had a new addict and his name was Johnny Dyess.

After his football glory days were behind him, Johnny sought another wondrous feeling, one that would leave him happy, even if numb to the world around him. He became enmeshed in a drug culture. Meth had made Johnny feel better than he ever felt drinking beer or smoking marijuana.

Consequences? They weren't considered. Johnny was so infatuated with his new drug choice, so reliant on it, that the Devil probably considered selling his soul to Johnny in hopes he could experience such a feeling.

"It was powerful stuff," Johnny said. "He had some of that in a little rock… red… so pure. At that time, we snorted it. After that, we smoked it in a glass tube. I did that and, whew, it was nothing like cocaine. Zoom! It gave you such a rush. What a feeling!"

Johnny had reached the destination where a good man had gone wrong, even if he was far from being the first such good egg to shatter.

The Red Crank Guy had Johnny completely hooked on the drug; Johnny had become completely dependent on the Red Crank Guy's product.

Supply and demand were at work.

The guy found another method of getting the drug and Johnny was so hooked he made a willing partner in whatever it took for the guy to make the drug.

The guy told Johnny they'd begin getting larger batches of the drug – "hardcore red crank" – in a pre-made form, so they wouldn't be subjected to running from store to store buying the necessary ingredients, particularly pseudoephedrine.

The plan seemed simple enough.

The two would drive to nearby Dothan, the largest city in the Wiregrass Area, rent a car, then drive northeast to Atlanta.

Perhaps they rented a car so they didn't use their own vehicles, perhaps it was to look like tourists, or perhaps it was to arrive in Atlanta without car trouble.

A four-door sedan, the usual choice, would suffice, because they could ride comfortably with plenty of room to store their cache – and weapons – on their return trip.

Whatever the reason, life became more complicated.

They used their three-hour drive from Dothan to Atlanta to get in "tough guy" mode. That included Johnny getting his gun ready, just in case their drug transactions went awry.

Johnny's friend had discovered some folks, "bad dudes" Johnny recalled. They had a large-scale meth operation in a downtown Atlanta warehouse. He called it a "real operation," and with it came very real danger. While the guy made the deal for the product, Johnny watched nearby armed with a small automatic rifle, complete, he said, with a 30-round clip.

The warehouse was near Hartsfield-Jackson Airport on the south side of Georgia's capital city, in an industrial area, some three or four blocks off main roads, Johnny recalled. The operation was solid, with 10-15 people usually there manufacturing methamphetamine. They wore white jackets; after all, they were in a laboratory. They wore masks, to avoid inhaling dangerous chemicals.

Johnny said the place was so clean you really couldn't detect the presence of meth. There was no smoke and the entire warehouse was only about the size, Johnny recalled as "half a gymnasium."

"Those guys knew I was armed," Johnny said. "I'd go just inside of the door while he (Red Crank Guy) would go with his guy to make the deal. That was probably the most dangerous point. I was armed, so I didn't care. They were armed, and they probably didn't care that I was armed. I'd hide the gun down in my back, but I'm pretty sure they had someone watching me. It seemed worth it at the time.

"My job was if something happened to him I was supposed to knock them down with my gun and get us out of there. I don't know what would have happened if something had gone down. I really didn't care. My main concern was to get him in there and get what he was supposed to get and then get back. It was something like out of the Breaking Bad shows. But, it wasn't a mom and pop operation. They were making chunks of the finished product there. If we'd had that all the time we'd be dead. It was strong."

Fortunately, the "guys" in Atlanta were good with Johnny and his partner… as long as the money arrived with them, as it always did. Had things turned bad, Johnny's not sure anyone was truly ready for "that kind of trouble. I sure hoped that I wouldn't have to use the gun."

The two from Alabama made the trip to Atlanta for meth some half-dozen times, going almost monthly. Johnny was paid off with drugs from the Red Crank Guy. They would return the rental car to Dothan, transfer the meth to their vehicles, and head back to Coffee County.

Johnny was ready to light up again, and as far as he knew, no one was the wiser. "That's just the power that stuff had on me," Johnny says. "It was powerful."

Johnny said Red Crank Guy was eventually set up by his son after a day of installing vinyl siding on a house. Johnny figures his partner had cut his son off from either his money or drugs… or both. So, the son placed a bag of marijuana under the seat in his father's personal truck. When Red Crank Guy returned from work, he got to his own truck and headed to Opp, where en route, tipped-off law enforcement waited and pulled him over. "He got busted way before I did." Johnny said. "He got locked up and I never saw him again. The son disappeared, too."

Johnny's connection was now behind bars, which meant he had to find a new method of getting meth.

"I had to start making it," Johnny said. "I had to learn."

He learned well.

Dyess family photo

Several of Alabama's Wishbone Boys reunited in Orange Beach
to help with the upcoming documentary. Pictured are (from left)
former quarterback Steadman Shealy, Gary Bramblett, Johnny
Dyess, former 5-time All-Pro center Dwight Stephenson, and
former NFL guard Buddy Aydelette.

Dyess family photo
Current Alabama head coach Nick Saban poses with
Johnny Dyess during an A-Club event.

Dyess family photo
Johnny Dyess gets a rarity, sitting behind Nick Saban's desk
at the University of Alabama.

Dyess family photo
Johnny Dyess instructs his Pee Wee offense during a 2012 game.

Chapter 16

CHASING A TAIL

FOOTBALL HAD BEEN Johnny's love. He maintained very good grades, but make no mistake about it, performing on Friday nights with Elba on his chest meant more to him than anything... even girls. It was that unconditional love for the sport that kept Johnny from finding another addiction.

The desire to play at his beloved Alabama, the same place his uncle had starred and where the "Bear" still roamed the sidelines kept any occasional happenstance on weekends with his friends from becoming a bad habit.

He had partied with friends on occasional weekends while in high school, mostly just drinking beer, but even then, "Not a lot," he said. "Because of sports, I kept it to a weekend deal. I probably hadn't dealt with marijuana because of sports. And even the beer was just on some Friday nights after a game, maybe at times on Saturday night. Football really kept me away from a lot of the drugs. That was my love. That overcame any addiction. It was the driving force even for going to class and making the grades... in high school and in college."

Johnny had grown up in a strong Southern Christian home. Not only were Percy and Clara Ann Dyess strong in their church – Percy was an elder at Westside Baptist Church – but they had both been educators. "They raised me in such a way I was always a good guy," Johnny said in the most matter-of-fact way. "I had made good grades. I had all A's through high school. Heck, I was a straight-A student, went to church, involved in church, involved in a lot of stuff."

As if Percy and Clara Ann weren't strong enough an influence, Johnny grandparents, on his mother's side, lived across Smith Avenue from him well into his adulthood. He was very close to them, too.

Things began to escalate after his football days ended. No longer devoted to anything, even a marriage and a stepdaughter, as devoted as he had been to football, Johnny tried losing himself in alcohol, then marijuana.

The only drug Johnny considered hardcore at the time he had tried it was cocaine, but he didn't like its short-time high. Pills were an entirely different problem. "I never was a pill guy," he said. "I never liked to take pills because I never knew what they were going to do to me. I'd seen other people and how they'd function on pills and they were just out of control. You just lose control of your body. You don't really know when it's going to take effect and you don't really know when it's going to wear off."

"It's like chasing a tail," Johnny said. "You'll never find that first hit again."

Chapter 17

‹‹‹ ❧ ›››

Origins of Meth

JOHNNY HAD FOUGHT hurtling down the highway to hell and back until he simply couldn't fight it any longer. He was on cruise control, and driving to Atlanta or any number of other locations to get more product to produce more meth became second nature. He had succumbed to its control. He was hooked.

Methamphetamine, tragically, has a lengthy history of forcing people into making bad decisions.

Meth's birth is argued from the middle of the 20th century to as far back as the late 1800s. Hell's Angels, Adolph Hitler and even a Japanese chemist are credited for the drug in some form or fashion.

As early as 1887, ephedrine was extracted from ephedra shrubs as a cough and asthma medication. By 1919, a Japanese chemist used ephedrine to produce a stimulant he named methamphetamine used initially for asthma, depression, narcolepsy and obesity.

The drug was marketed in Germany to the public as an all-purpose "upper" that beat back everything from depression to hay fever.

Reportedly, German Führer Adolph Hitler had his scientists develop the drug to increase his Nazi soldiers' ability to stay up for several days. Pervitin, a form of methamphetamine, is credited in some circles as the reason German successfully beat France's armed forces in World War II. Hitler physician Theodor Morell had won the Führer's confidence in 1936 by curing his longtime stomach pain, but Morell's drug is also credited for prolonging the war.

Some scientists say it was closer to what today is known as methamphetamine. Others say it was oxycodone, and some say it was morphine. Still others believe it was a combination of all three.

Regardless, even Hitler was reported to have become a meth junkie.

Norman Ohler, a German writer, authored a book – *Blitzed: Drugs in the Third Reich* – about Nazis using meth. Soldiers fatigued during WWII were given the drug by German medical officers. It was placed on the soldiers' tongues, gulped down with water, and the fighting for Hitler's army continued without more breaks for lengthy periods of time.

Nazi scientists performed experiments on Jewish inmates by forcing them to march in circles without sleep and determining whether cocaine or the new drug was a better stimulant. Using drugs to fight a war is alive and well today as Islamic fighters have reportedly used the meth derivative Captagon in 2014. It was said to have reduced fighters' fears and was especially good for suicide missions.

The drug eventually made its way to America, where soldiers and pilots were exposed to it through emergency medical kits in the mid-1940's.

By the 1960's, the drug was being used by doctors in San Francisco to treat heroin addicts' dependency. It may have caused more damage than good.

Crystal meth began production in the late 1970's, focusing on the extraction of ephedrine or pseudoephedrine from cough medicines. Recipes included such ingredients as antifreeze, battery acid, drain cleaners and paint thinners. Hell's Angels and other biker gangs began marketing crystal meth, mainly on the west coast.

Among extremes methamphetamine users will venture to make

sure they'll be able to get their "next" high, include filtering their own urine. Law enforcement officers have found bottles of urine at residences where users reside.

A large amount of the drug is disposed from the body through urine, and a filtering system can save some of the chemicals for reuse. It is a method known as urine extraction, and hard-core meth addicts collect their urine, or even that of other users, consuming it to get the high from the drug still in the urine.

Johnny was never that desperate. He didn't need to go to such an extreme; he was so good at cooking the drug, and despite his constant use, he maintained a respectable physical appearance. Nevertheless, he certainly went other distances chasing his high.

Regardless of tax bracket, meth addicts often unite in filth and squalor. What was once a natural affinity for living with a clean body, even a relatively clean house and general maintenance of one's appearance, are no longer priorities … not even a concern.

Items begin piling up, akin to someone with dementia stacking pots and pans and glasses, usually dirty, for weeks, maybe even months.

Residences of those addicted to the drug are typically ridden with filth, dangerous filth. Coffee County Sheriff's Chief Deputy Ronnie Whitworth recalled an instance when a meth lab was busted at a residence with 13 microwaves lined along a bar to increase the cooking process. At the end of the bar was a young child eating cereal.

On other occasions, residences have been found with active meth labs and young children present, but no food to be found. Priorities, needless to say, are altered.

Johnny maintained his home and generally kept to himself, aside from occasional visits to his parents and a few friends that stopped by.

Whitworth said the one thing he's found common at many meth residences has been some type of collection, such as Johnny's coin collection. Some have what most would classify as bizarre sex toys. Others are into pornography.

Mood changes are something law enforcement look for with

suspected drug users. Whitworth recalled one of the first times he encountered a meth addict in the 1990's. A woman had pulled up to Whitworth's unit, saying somebody was after her and she was afraid to drive to her house.

Whitworth told her he would follow her to make sure she and the young child in the back seat got home safely. As he began to follow the woman, she began speeding, exceeding 120 miles-per-hour. When they got to her residence, the woman was arrested. Somewhere along the way, she thought in her mind the law was the "bad guy" chasing her.

"I remember when I was police chief and went to a conference where a guy was talking about meth," Whitworth said. "He said, 'If you've never heard of it, you're going to. It's coming.' He was right."

Little did Whitworth know it would hit so close to home… very close.

It is believed some 35 million people on the planet use meth, with as much as one-third of those living in America.

Methamphetamine releases a sudden surge of dopamine, a chemical responsible for pleasure in the brain. Dopamine, naturally produced by the body, can even result from eating.

Cigarettes, drugs and alcohol release dopamine in uncommonly high levels. Meth stimulating the release of excess dopamine, heightens the feeling of pleasure. Meth triggers dopamine in "reward" areas of the brain, giving users a rush. It is about 10 times the normal dopamine delivered.

The problem is dopamine has only so much in reserve and users sometimes drain these reserves. More use only damages the body's ability to produce more dopamine. Once the level is diminished in a body, ensuing dosages of meth do not deliver the same rush as previously.

Staying alert and getting a mental boost is nothing new for mankind. Ancient Chinese were said to have received their kicks from má huáng, a tea brewed from an ephedra-producing shrub. South Americans ingest yerba mate from small gourds. Somalis chew khat.

Daily, around the globe, people are getting a boost by smoking cigarettes for the nicotine, drinking coffee for the caffeine, and eating chocolate for the sugar. Legal amphetamines in the form of Adderall or Ritalin are heavily prescribed in the United States and other developed nations to treat ADHD in school-age children.

Once processed, meth becomes a stimulant drug that can be taken as a pill, smoked through a glass pipe, snorted, or injected intravenously after it has been dissolved in water/alcohol.

Crystal methamphetamine has the appearance of glass fragments or shiny rocks. Other names for the drug include crank, crystal, ice, chalk, speed, glass, blade, shards, Shabu and Tina.

The meth high has been reported to never be as good for the user after the first time, and users are chasing that feeling each time after initial use. The high does not tend to be long-lived, and repeated doses are especially dangerous.

Users can overdose on meth, even have a stroke, heart attack or organ problems.

Short-term effects include staying awake for abnormal periods, increased wakefulness, decreased appetite, faster breathing, rapid and/or irregular heartbeat, and increased blood pressure and body temperature.

As for long-term effects, aside from the obvious risks of contracting HIV and/or hepatitis B and C with intravenous methods, meth users usually don't make sound decisions, leading to risky behaviors, such as unprotected sex. Meth does increase a user's sex drive and decreases inhibition.

Long-time meth users can experience extreme weight loss, dental problems, such as tooth decay and what is known as "meth mouth," intense itching (leading to skin lesions from scratching), anxiety, confusion, sleep problems, violent behavior, paranoia and hallucinations.

Chemicals from meth can be excreted through the skin via perspiration, which damages the skin, producing sores on many meth users' faces. Some of these sores are self-inflicted. Restricted blood vessels caused by the drug make users scratch, almost non-stop.

Delusions will have users believing bugs are crawling under their skin.

Meth Mouth results from the drug causing rapid tooth decay. The acidic nature of meth and the lack of saliva causing dry mouth, leave teeth highly vulnerable, especially when users with poor dental hygiene frequently eat sweets to excess. It's a combination producing serious after-effects, sometimes taking just a few weeks for users to become completely different personalities.

A post-use effect, particularly in binge meth users, can cause what is commonly known as tweaking. Euphoria is replaced with paranoia, irritability, restlessness, hallucination and delusion. Users eventually crash, during which time they can experience a period of depression and fatigue.

Withdrawal from the drug can also cause problems, such as anxiety, fatigue, severe depression, psychosis and intense craving for more drugs. The drug gives the rush anywhere from 4 to 12 hours, depending on the user.

Anxiety caused by meth will often have users feeling they are in danger, although they are unsure why. A person's emotional anxiety is triggered by meth use. Paranoia hits about 80 percent of meth users within the first few months of using. In many cases, violence is associated with meth. Paranoia and delusions from the use of meth can lead to homicide.

Meth can damage the brain, but that can be reversed after a user has been off the drug for an unspecified period of time. Other damages may be ever-lasting effects, such as affecting motor skills or the development of Parkinson's disease. Meth is said to remain in a body's circulation far longer than cocaine, which only increases many of its side effects.

Studies have also found meth abusers and addicts have a decrease in a protein called BDNF, which normally provides protection in the brain by helping nerve cells grow, reach maturity and stay in good working order.

Meth initially causes a user to have a spiritual bond, but that is short-lived as faith eventually fades, even if they feel they're suddenly braver, stronger, smarter and sexier.

One of the best descriptions of the drug compares it to a loan shark. The borrowed high does not last long, and a user's valuable resources are soon grabbed by the drug. Soon, the user is unable to meet the loan shark's demands. Hopelessness and depression appear.

There are treatments, the best considered behavioral therapies, but there are currently no government-approved medications to treat methamphetamine addiction.

Dan Ledford, executive director of Transform Seminars in Dothan, who had Johnny as a guest speaker at one of his events, said not doing anything to help those addicted to meth is akin to putting a Band-Aid on cancer. "If we don't do something, that's exactly what we'd be doing for these people."

New laws on the books have helped curb the problem. NPLEx is a tracking system used by law enforcement that monitors the sale of a key meth ingredient – pseudoephedrine medication. NPLEx has been in place at all pharmacies in Alabama since 2012, when Alabama's Legislature passed some of the toughest anti-meth legislation in the country. Alabama's legislation has since become a model for other states as they work combat methamphetamine production, while still allowing easy access to crucial allergy medications.

Chapter 18

— ∿ —

BECOMING A MASTER COOK

NOW THAT THE Red Crank Guy had disappeared, Johnny was forced to find his meth from a new source. He tried buying homemade manufactured meth locally, but it wasn't up to his standards.

There was meth being made in Johnny's area, but he had become picky in his choice of quality and no one, he said, made it as good, as clean, as he preferred. "But, they were trying to make money," he said, noting cutting here and there in production kept quality down. "Over a period of time, that's what led me into start making it."

In 1999, Johnny began manufacturing meth at his house on Morrow Street. "It actually went on all right, although I didn't know what I was doing," he said. "I paid somebody to come show me what to do. I paid 'em a certain amount of money and gave them a portion of the finished product. I had watched closely and I got pretty good at it. I wanted all my stuff good."

The best way to obtain pseudoephedrine for manufacturing was by purchasing the cold medicine Sudafed. Johnny still had to purchase pseudoephedrine, and those buys were becoming tougher as law enforcement began limiting pharmacies on how much one could purchase.

He was working construction, usually in the Florida Panhandle, building canopies for a chain of convenience stores. He would purchase Sudafed at different stores in Crestview, Niceville, Milton, and of course spread it around back home in Elba, Enterprise and other localities.

"To begin with, you could just buy all the Sudafed you wanted," Johnny said. "To start with, I'd just go to Walmart or Rite-Aid or anywhere like that. It was on the counter then. You'd go get a box at Walmart, go get a box at CVS, go get a box at Rite-Aid, go to Troy and go to Walmart, Rite Aid and CVS. I don't think the stores cared back then, really. I tried to space it out where I wasn't at a one store so often. I was trying to dodge getting noticed by the law, so I'd go to Florida sometimes. They eventually got wind of me."

He said emergence of the internet changed everything, and was soon used as an information source for law enforcement. Johnny would have to adjust, changing his buying tactics.

New laws required a signature when buying Sudafed, so there wouldn't be an over-purchase of the drug.

Obtaining required meth ingredients became quite a problem for those manufacturing the drug. Without proper ingredients, a recipe is useless.

Johnny had eager customers that wanted his product and would gladly buy pseudophedrine for him, if they could get some of his finished product.

"If other people got it for me we did a trade out," he said. "I had all of the formulas for everything, how much they'd get if they brought me this amount or that amount. I knew how to make it and the cook would always get half of the product. Maybe somebody would give me just a little bit and they'd get one-half of one-third. That was the only way they were going to get any finished product from me because the money is really what I needed. And, If I needed a little money I could always sell a little bit."

While pharmacies and other chemical suppliers will sell phosphorus, a vital ingredient in the recipe for meth, to customers with a driver's license and signature, Johnny easily beat that system by the oh-so-slow method of getting it from matches.

Buying matches was no problem as he would just go into one of the stores where he was working and load up on them.

Phosphorus is on the tip – striking end – of a match. It takes a lot of matches to produce enough phosphorus used in the cooking of meth. It takes about 20,000 matchbooks to get 100 grams of phosphorus, and 20,000 matches cost about $600.

Of course, then comes the time-consuming separation of phosphorus from matches, leaving as little cardboard – the holding end of the match – as possible. The remainder is then submerged in acetone to dissolve the glue holding phosphorus to the cardboard. The remnants are then filtered so any cardboard remains are removed. The phosphorus is purified with acetone, boiled with hydrochloric acid, then distilled water. It is filtered again and dried.

While Johnny didn't want meth's full recipe disclosed, he worked around the pseudoephedrine and phosphorus. He also learned where to purchase crystallized iodine, and learned the proper amounts of everything to make the drug. "When I was in it I knew all the math tables," he said.

"I called what I made the old way of cooking," Johnny said. "I thought it was dangerous, but the way they do it today is a lot more dangerous."

Johnny set up his meth manufacturing business behind his house in a small building he'd built. It was almost always active, never being "down" for more than a week, two tops.

Nevertheless, he'd perfected both the art of buying ingredients, as well as the art of cooking the product. "Oh, I was good at it," he said. "Oh yeah. I was pretty much making it for myself, but I was real good at it after four or five years. I'd pretty much perfected it."

Soon, laws were changed to limit the amount of pseudoephedrine that could be purchased by an individual in a month, and it didn't matter where you bought it, Florida, Alabama, anywhere.

Johnny tried dodging the system again, but to no avail. He believes new technology is "probably what did me in and getting the law to my house. It wasn't the actual manufacturing of it that brought them to my house. It was the buying of the pills. That's what led them to me."

Johnny sold very little of his finished product, although people that knew about his meth tried to buy some. He usually only sold it if he needed to buy more product to make more meth.

He would usually cook on the weekends and take enough meth with him to work in Florida during the week. "I'm sure my construction bosses knew a little bit what was going on with me, because none of them really did it," Johnny said. "I smoked it when I'd go to the bathroom. It had a little bit of odor, but you could do it and go undetected, pretty much."

There were others in the area manufacturing meth, too, but on an even smaller scale than Johnny. Wouldn't one large batch last a while? "You'd think so," he said. "But, it wasn't always a big batch because I couldn't get all of the ingredients."

Where Johnny once thought about gaining big yardage on 31 traps or taking out a blitzing middle linebacker in pass protection, he now spent his waking hours either figuring out how to get his next supply of pseudoephedrine so he could cook another batch of meth, or making preparations to cook his next batch.

Money, as rare as paydays were becoming, was surprisingly not a concern.

"Yeah, I never really thought about that," he says. "A job was, psst… I didn't need a job. I had everything I wanted. I didn't really need any money. If I did, I could sell a little bit. I'd pick up odd jobs here and there and do a little job for someone that I knew. I always seemed to have money. It was always there."

Johnny had perfected the art of getting by. He just wasn't a perfect soul. Far from it, in fact.

"I didn't really care about a future long as I had some meth," he said. "As long as I had some around, I really didn't care about much of nothin'."

There was one memorable party where everyone had started going hard early, mainly drinking beer. It was late in the evening and people were slowing down, some even ready to sleep. One guy asked, "Why is Johnny not as tired as us?" A friend who knew what Johnny had taken told them, "He's on a different program than us."

Chapter 19

ECSTASY AND AGONY

JOHNNY HAD ACCUMULATED quite a large coin collection over the years. It was his hobby. When drugs took over his life, the collection all but ended, but he still had the coins to occupy his time. Well, kinda.

Johnny had developed an interest in collecting coins, specifically wheat pennies, at some point. His father had shared some of his older coins, and Johnny began looking for different mints on coins.

Johnny was rarely working a regular job, so often, while at home, he'd get high by himself. When drug-induced euphoria had him feeling good, he sometimes placed his coin collection on his coffee table, pulling it close to him. He would get out his magnifying glasses to take a closer look at the coins.

Johnny would plan on counting each coin, going through each one and documenting them. He would begin sorting the coins into categories. That would last for only a short while, 10, maybe 20 coins, before Johnny began coming down from his high. "That's when I'd get my stuff back out to start smoking meth again," he said. "I'd never get back to messing with the coins. They always got pushed to the side."

The process was repeated often as the coins sat in a container next to Johnny's couch. He never made it very far.

"I've still got most all of them," he said. "I never really got through going through them. Little things like that. You wanted to do stuff and it'd give you a boost wanting to do something, but in the back of your mind you're thinking, 'When I start coming down I've got some more, so I'll do some more. If it was really good, it was like you wanted to stay up and it was hard to lay down. I knew I was as high as I was gonna get, but it was hard to lay it down and even enjoy it because it was just there and you always thought you needed more."

The euphoria caused by the drug hardly cured all ills for Johnny. Rather, it multiplied them. He thought he couldn't do without it. Countless times he thought he would quit; he thought he could quit. Usually, those times occurred when the drug supply was running low.

Johnny was always going to straighten up.

"I never really had a plan in place to manufacture some more or have a good source to go get some," he said. "Maybe I had been on a long run of it and I just kind of felt wore out from it. I had a feeling that I kinda wanted to do something better with my life, and when this batch was gone I was gonna try to make a change. I'm gonna try to do without it."

The unfunny joke was on Johnny. He had no such power.

"Some would come along," he said. "I'd find a way. It would take a few days of sleep and rest but I'd find a way to come up with some more supplies."

Usually, when Johnny had been making meth for himself and suddenly ran out, it meant he was out of supplies to make more. It also usually meant he didn't have the means to get more supplies. However, someone would almost always come through with either their meth supply for Johnny or pseudoephedrine to help him manufacture more.

"I'd get enough to get me going again where I would go out," he said. "It is such a vicious cycle that you get caught up in. You don't want to run out, number one. You know that down feeling. It's a bad feeling. You don't have the energy to do anything. You're going so fast; you're going here and there and here and there so fast, then it's like somebody just jerked the bottom out from under you, and that fall is hard. Usually, to get up from that fall, eventually you had to do some more meth to get back up. My body would just be craving it and my mind thought I had to have it.

"It just made you feel like you wanted to get up and move around and do something. The negative part of it was that you'd start a lot of stuff but you couldn't stay focused long enough to finish anything. Your body will shut down sooner or later. I've been on the couch and been doing it and would fall asleep and wake up with the lighter in one hand and maybe a glass tube in the other and it rolled off onto the floor. I always wrapped it up in a towel so it wouldn't get smut on it or so it wouldn't break. You really took care of it.

You'd be sitting there and the effect it gave you, there shouldn't have been any way you could go to sleep. But, you've been on it so long and you hadn't had any sleep. I've probably been up 3 or 4 days. After the third day you really don't know what's going on. You can't function too well. You're doing what they call wiggin' out. You can't comprehend anything. You're just there. A clock means nothing… night or day, doesn't mean anything. Your TV runs solid. You could tell the time of day by what was on TV. The only thing that meant anything was if you had more to use."

Johnny's friends, on occasion, would stop in if they drove past his house and saw his light on in the den. It was usually only those in Johnny's inner circle that would visit. They would sit around and talk until another sun rose from the east.

"We'd talk about getting high," Johnny said. "'How much more you got? Got any you want to get rid of?' It was never anything constructive. We'd smoke pot, too. Pot really worked against the meth. But we liked that feeling, too. So, really the ultimate high for us was to smoke the meth and get that good energetic feeling, then roll a blunt and walk outside and smoke it. If it was during the day we'd go outside and talk about stuff we were gonna do. You were always gonna do something but you never finish anything. That's the sad part of that."

Johnny was getting by simply because he didn't need money for material things, and he went to his parents' house to eat. Yes, he lost weight on meth, but not many people noticed because he made himself eat. He did some painting jobs and worked other odd jobs, including selling scrap metal. "I was pretty happy most of the time," he said. "But, I did lose my wife and my job."

Early one morning – Johnny only knew that it was dark outside – he awoke with his Jeep buried nose-first in a ditch, at about 5 a.m. He was on the opposite side of the road from the direction he'd been heading and, to this day, he's uncertain if it happened in Coffee County or Covington County – "It was in the middle of nowhere," he said. He awoke just enough to know his back wheels were off the ground and he wasn't going to be able to move the vehicle. To heck with it, he thought, and he climbed over to the passenger's seat and fell asleep.

When the sun rose, Johnny exited the Jeep and flagged down a passerby who pulled the Jeep out; Johnny promptly drove home and again fell asleep.

While on meth, or just a common drunk, Johnny said he often drove through intersections and people's yards. He'd realize what he had done, but just kept driving until he reached his destination, which was home.

"I really didn't get out and travel that much," Johnny said. "Now the alcohol, that was a different story. When you drink the first thing you want to do is get in your car and go somewhere. In my case, I drank mostly beer. There ain't no telling how much I'd drink, a case at least. My Daddy once said, 'Johnny would be alright on that beer, but when he drinks one he thinks he's got to drink all of them.' And that's pretty much the way it was. One was too many and 100 was never enough."

In late 2007, Johnny was pulled over by law enforcement at a road block after work. It was about 10 p.m. and he was driving a company truck owned by the construction group that had hired him.

He'd been given the job by a friend of his parents. He lost that job because of the subsequent stop. Johnny had that DUI charge on deferred prosecution and was only about a month away from its being dissolved, but officers at the road block smelled marijuana. That presented an entirely new set of problems.

Ironically, Johnny had been unable to find his insurance card in a timely manner, giving officers on hand a whiff of pot. "I would have got through it if I'd found the insurance card," he said. "They pulled me over to the side and said they smelled it. So, then they went to searching. Everything else was in my bag."

The road block had been directly in front of the former location of Kleinert's.

Johnny always thought he'd get away with any legal issues. After all, he said, "The number of times I didn't get caught outweighed the number of times I got caught."

He quit drinking for the most part when he began manufacturing meth. "I didn't want to, but I knew that drinking and driving, I was going to get in trouble," he said.

Then came rock bottom. Johnny was sick and he knew it deep down in his gut. He hated the way he was living. "I just didn't know how to quit on my own. I wasn't strong enough to quit. That's what it takes. You've gotta get to the bottom."

Johnny had arrived.

Chapter 20

———— ❧ ————

I Do… More Than You Know

Johnny loved his family. He loved his friends. He loved football. He loved his dog. He thought he loved his meth, but the drug was cheating on him, and he discovered as much when it was almost too late.

He went about things as if his priorities were in proper order, including his job, well, that is until meth took over. He lost his wife and stepdaughter. He lost his job. While incarcerated, he lost the chance of being around his parents. He even lost his dog. Only meth remained constant, and while in jail, that too was lost.

The joys of having a few beers with his buddies had evolved. Some may say it had festered. Meanwhile, his life was dissolving.

Johnny doesn't even remember whose house he first tried the red crank, but he certainly recalls having to go home to his wife. "That wasn't pretty," he said. "When I went home, I couldn't go to sleep. She knew something was different. She was on a rampage. 'What have you been doing? I know you've been doing something.' I'd say, 'No. We were just drinking.' She knew it was something more than that. I saw real quick that I wasn't going to be able to hide that from her. I had to figure out a way. I'd hidden smoking pot from her. I don't know how, but I did. I thought I was anyway."

Drug use, which led to financial woes, sent his life spiraling downward. He spent lots of money on drugs, but he always needed more.

Johnny began smoking, rather than snorting the red crank. An added bonus, the high lasted longer for him that way. "I really liked the feeling," he said. "I had not liked the burning in my nose from snorting. When I learned how to smoke it, that became my choice."

Somewhere, Johnny's mind truly believed he was not like the others. Maybe he wasn't. Even multiple arrests, the loss of career-potential jobs, slamming of cell doors behind him, and the embarrassment he had of disappointing his parents worse than any nightmare he had ever sweated through, Johnny still thought he was different.

Turns out, he was right. It only took him the better part of two decades to prove it.

The grip methamphetamine has on its victims is a mighty one. And no matter what he thought, Johnny wasn't going to quit. It's so life consuming that it's hard to imagine anyone that's used it very much could ever give it up without being physically separated from it, be it death or imprisonment. With the depths Johnny had fallen to, he was destined for one or the other.

Anyone that saw Johnny during his days as a user, regardless of whether they had known him beforehand, could tell he had a glazed look in his eyes, a far-away look. Law enforcement will often say of junkies, "The lights are on, but nobody's home." That was Johnny.

All of this despite an upbringing that had molded a heart of gold in Johnny. He had tried so bad to be so good.

He had figured meth was better than drinking. After all, he said, he had, for the most part, stopped drinking. He would find bottles sitting around full that he had opened. His attention was always on the drug and making more, smoking more. Also, the DUIs would stop if he was not driving, and meth kept him home much more than had alcohol.

"If you're home drinking, the first thing you want to do is get in your car and go somewhere," he said. "The only problem if you did go somewhere after using, you couldn't go far without wanting to stop and do it again. I didn't care to go anywhere while I was on meth. I wanted to stay home and keep it all to myself."

Chapter 21

$\sim$

METHIN' AROUND

JOHNNY WAS IN the proverbial hand basket and he was headed straight to Satan's front porch. The only question was where he'd end up first – in prison or in a casket.

His thoughts were consumed by meth; when to smoke, when to make it, when to buy more product to make some more, when to smoke some more.

"It makes you make bad decisions," he said. "I thought meth was the cure all (for) my problems. I didn't drink any more. But, you're never out. I was 49 and I was far from out. If I wanted to do something I pretty much just did it and suffered the consequences and whatever came with it."

Johnny no longer had a wife or a beautiful stepdaughter. He really had no true friends, only those that looked at him as a chance to get high. His parents were there for him, but they knew. They had to. Their son just wasn't going anywhere. And regardless of how hard he tried to hide his habit, there were signs. There had to be.

Johnny's lived in Elba for most of his life. His teenage years were normal.

It'd started with a little beer, then a little marijuana. After a four-year stay in Tuscaloosa, he returned home, older and looking to fill a void football had filled.

He moved briefly in Opp with his wife and stepdaughter who'd entered his life, but soon after, so did meth. Eventually, Johnny was alone with just the meth to keep him company.

Meth made Johnny feel uninhibited. Though never shy, he was no longer the quiet guy he'd been. Only now, he felt 10-feet tall and bullet-proof. "You think there ain't nothing you can't do and you don't worry about consequences. That's the lure of it. Plus, it masked any other feelings you might have, such as girlfriend problems, job problems, money problems, stuff like that."

Getting by, day-by-day was Johnny's main purpose, his goal. With that meant the cycle of taking and making meth over and over again.

Johnny should've had a problem with his parents, who lived nearby. He had to at least look and act normally around them. He always had answers for whatever they'd ask, but they seldom asked. He made himself eat at least once per day to maintain some semblance of a healthy body, although his only true craving was meth.

"You do what you gotta do," he said, referring to visiting his parents regularly. "I'd go and stay for whatever time I could. Normally, I'd get little bit high before I went. If had it, I was doing it anyway. And I'd just leave when I needed to.

"Meth is kinda like water. If you start drinking it and like it, if it's there you're gonna drink it. It becomes such a crutch. You become reliant on it to function. That's why you don't ever want to run out. You might stay off it a little bit, but don't want to run out."

After the Red Crank Guy was busted, Johnny had been forced to make it or find another supplier. He'd chosen to not only make it, but to perfect cooking it.

For a while, Johnny had driven his father's pickup, a 1992 Chevrolet. When he picked up his last DUI, he was driving a Jeep. Johnny called his father from jail and said, "Daddy, if you'll get me out, you can have it. I didn't even have a license."

By 1996, Percy and Clara Ann purchased the house where Johnny honed his "cooking" skills. It was only a little more than a mile from their home.

"My first experience was such a high, such a rush," he said. "I had a lot of energy, but I couldn't control myself. I'd start 50 projects but never finish one. When you're using, most of the time it's with friends, but it's a selfish drug. You want to save every little bit for yourself. When you run out, you gotta go on the hunt. You don't know where you're next (drug) is coming from."

Since meth use made him stay home when he was holding, there was Johnny, with all his past Friday night glory, making his hometown proud as a member of some of "Bear" Bryant's greatest teams at Alabama, just hanging out at his little house.

Memorabilia many collectors would go great distances to obtain was scattered about, ready to be stored somewhere, or perhaps even taken to a dumpster. It may have meant something at some point to Johnny, but not now. Not while he had meth to make… and take.

With the highs came sleep deprivation, sometimes for extended periods. "I don't care who you are, when you're up three or four days straight with no sleep you get tired," he said.

He was heading down a road of destruction, quite a dirty one indeed. Yet, he didn't know where the road was leading him.

"Meth is the work of the devil," Johnny acknowledges today. "It was tough on my parents, but they never gave up on me. But, I lost it all because of drugs. I lost my job because of poor job performance, but my poor job performance was because of drugs."

Chapter 22

ANGELS IN BLACK

Dyess family photo
Johnny with a young Cinnamon at his home on Morrow Street in Elba.

Dyess family photo
Johnny's parents helped him get this house on Morrow Street in
Elba. He and a friend were standing on the front porch the day
"black angels" came to rescue him.

FOR A DOZEN years as a user and most of that as a meth cook, Johnny avoided major brushes with the law. That all changed in 2008 when he'd driven up on a road block in Coffee County.

Officers found drug paraphernalia in Johnny's vehicle, which happened to be the company truck. He was promptly carried off to the Coffee County Jail.

Johnny was released a short while later; he returned home and almost immediately began perfecting his craft of cooking meth.

While God had made his appearance often in Johnny's life, so had Satan. The good was obvious, but the bad was there, too.

His parents had provided him a house. It was certainly nothing special; two bedrooms, small office area, a living area, a kitchen, dining room and a bathroom. There was a small front porch, and a separate building out back Johnny had built. He would perfect his art of cooking methamphetamine in that building. It was all he needed.

Johnny knew to keep the house clean. If he didn't, his parents would come over more often to help him clean. The house was in both Johnny and his parents' names. The financial setup was a move Johnny believes his father needed to make. "It was a smart move," Johnny said. "He did that in case something happened to me. This way, (the authorities) couldn't take it." At the rate Johnny was going, something was bound to happen to him.

Johnny had called a friend, asking him if he wanted to hang out while he was drying a new batch of meth. Johnny cooked a batch almost every day then. He knew another guy with some marijuana, so he called and the guy delivered the pot.

The pot delivery guy hadn't been gone long when, around 3 p.m. on this Wednesday, Johnny and his buddy were goofing off, quite high at this point, on the front porch.

"It was a normal day," Johnny recalled, remember the date – July 29, 2009. "Me and my buddy were standing on the porch. He was fixin' to leave. We had just been talking. Then, we looked out and saw them black SUVs coming."

About two blocks up the road from his house, beside a cemetery, the SUVs appeared. "I said, 'Oh, looks like someone's gonna be in trouble," Johnny recalled, remembering how naïve he was thinking the Drug Task Force caravan was heading down the road to "get" a guy who'd been busted a couple of weeks earlier.

Things quickly changed from worse to worst.

A mere two months before having his latest charges cleared, Johnny and his friend watched six or seven black SUVs – he doesn't recall the exact number – turn down his dirt road. He knows there were enough to make quite a long line. "I'm sure more showed up once they found what they found," he said.

Regardless of the number, Johnny knew every one of the SUVs meant business. Their look was unmistakable.

"I knew it was law enforcement... Drug Task Force (DTF). I'd seen 'em before," Johnny said. "I knew what they looked like. Ain't no doubt who they are."

The SUVs represented not only members of the 12th Judicial Drug Task Force, but also members of the Coffee County Sheriff's Department. In fact, family friend and Coffee County Chief Deputy Ronnie Whitworth not only had been made aware of the impending operation, he led it!

"The investigators worked through me," Whitworth said. "They kept me informed. No rumors or anything of the operation could come out. I'm gonna do my job. We've got a policy that we deal with things as they come up. If the DTF wants help, I'll do everything I can to help out."

For so long Johnny had avoided prison. Could he get out of this? For Heaven's sake, the lab was still active out back. Things didn't look promising, but were they really coming for him?

Any naivety quickly vanished as the SUVs pulled up to the front of Johnny's house. He realized life as he knew it was over. What they were sure to find would be the final, final straw.

"They turned in and came right up my driveway," he said. "My heart just went.... (he placed his hands over his heart, recalling the sheer terror he faced that afternoon.) I knew then they'd come for me. There was nothing I could do at that point."

The black SUVs resembled the scene in the movie "Ghost," where ghouls appeared in black and took spirits away. Though Johnny didn't know it then, the black SUVs were taking away his demons.

Depending on the state of mind at the time, it can be difficult to tell the difference between an angel and a demon.

Johnny's friend tried to leave in his pickup, but he was detained. Johnny had stepped back into the house and closed the door. He opened it as soon as the DTF knocked.

"I didn't want them seeing (the lab), but of course, they said they smelled it," he said. "They might have, but I don't think they could smell any of it. They just knew about me."

Several members of the DTF had gone to the back of Johnny's house, in case other folks were on hand and trying to run. Johnny stepped out front, although he admits the fine details of the moment are cloudy, perhaps because of the pot, but more than likely because of his rattled nerves.

The DTF asked him if he had been sick. "I knew what they were getting at," Johnny said. "I said, 'Yeah, I had a cold.'"

Not skipping a beat, a member of the DTF replied, "Well, you must have had it for a long time."

The DTF agent asked Johnny if he was using meth at his residence or if he was buying the pseudoephedrine for someone else.

"I said, 'I'm actually getting it for someone else,'" Johnny replied.

The DTF wanted to search the house, but they had yet to acquire a warrant. Initially, Johnny thought about not letting the agents enter his home, but he knew they would just wait and get a search warrant soon enough. They pulled Johnny to the back of a vehicle and talked with him.

"I guess one thing led to another, and knowing there was nothing I could do, I just sat there and let 'em go in," Johnny said. "I even went in and showed 'em everything."

The meth lab was still active.

"Once I showed 'em what I had out there in the back it wasn't too long before they were carrying me to the car," he said. "I knew it wasn't gonna be no gettin' out soon. I guess really I thought, 'Well, it's about time.'"

The arrest meant the loss of several guns agents confiscated during the raid. Johnny didn't have to worry about losing a job. He didn't have one, outside of odd jobs here and there.

After being placed under arrest, his immediate concern was his dog, Cinnamon. "I was worried about her," he said. "My Mama and Daddy were out of town at the beach, so I didn't know what was gonna happen to her."

Johnny thought Whitworth had taken Cinnamon, but he'd called the local animal shelter to come get her. "Ronnie made sure she was alright," Johnny said. "Bless her heart, she's been run through the mill. She went through it, too. Unconditional love. She's been as faithful a companion to me and my parents as anyone."

Cinnamon would be with Johnny until she died years later at age 15.

Johnny was placed at "Blue Top," the Coffee County Jail, in New Brockton to the east. This time he had a $350,000 cash-only bond placed with his incarceration.

Black represents the unknown. It's the color of choice for funerals. It's considered colorless. While mentioned in the same breath as white, white represents the light. Johnny saw no light when the SUVs came up his driveway, only darkness. Truth is, he'd seen darkness long before the SUVs turned off Morrow Street and into his drive.

"Black Angels," as Johnny now refers to the SUVs, stopped his path to an almost certain premature death.

Seemingly, Johnny had reached the end of the line. What he could not realize then, facing so many felony charges, was it was the beginning of a better life.

His old dirt road has since been paved. That's all, just simple asphalt. But, to Johnny, there's no greater street on earth. Today, it's his jeweled road.

Chapter 23

—✽—

BLUE TOP BLUES

JOHNNY KNEW WHERE the Coffee County Jail was located. Heck, he knew its blueprint, probably, as well, perhaps even better than the contractor that built the place. He'd been an overnight guest at the jail, so to speak, on multiple occasions after being arrested. He knew the jailers as if they were family.

He'd grown up next door to Coffee County Sheriff's Office Chief Deputy Ronnie Whitworth, a close friend of the family. Whitworth had overseen the operation that brought Johnny in for his latest incarceration; his office was just steps away from the jail. Johnny even referred to Whitworth as "Brother Ronnie," the name he had begun calling Whitworth at church many years earlier.

Johnny referred to the jail as "Blue Top," the name given the complex by those that saw it from nearby Alabama Highway 84 due to its blue tin roofs that could be spotted with ease from far away.

This time, Blue Top would hardly be a weekend retreat for Johnny.

He had a list, quite a lengthy one at that, of charges and some were serious. The jail, located in New Brockton, was about 10 miles from his home in Elba; it might as well have been in Canada. This time it was colder at Blue Top. This time there was uncertainty of how long he'd be there or where he would go when he got out… if he got out. Prison was a strong possibility.

Whitworth had told Percy and Clara Ann the best thing they could do for their son was to allow tough love to come into play. It was not easy on Johnny, nor his parents, nor Whitworth, a man Johnny said, who "… has been a friend all of my life, even though he was an Auburn guy."

Whitworth lived next door to Percy and Clara Ann. "If you want to save Johnny's life, leave him in jail."

Johnny said it was obviously hard on him, but also was tough on his parents. Nevertheless, he understands it was the right thing to do. "Otherwise, I'd be dead right now," he said.

A meeting Whitworth had set up with Johnny and his parents in his office was planned by Whitworth to somehow shock Johnny into changing. It had worked. Johnny saw the handcuffs and shackles clearer than ever as they reflected in the eyes of his parents.

"That was the lowest," Johnny said. "I was hurt, broken. The only thing you talk about in jail is how can I get out of jail. But this was different. I knew then that reality had hit and something needed to change. Up that point, it was all about me getting out of jail, not changing, seriously changing. I was playing the game of fooling somebody. But, when Brother Ronnie told me the lifespan of a (meth) cook was six years and I knew I'd been doing 12 years, it hit home with me."

All three of them would be crying and sobbing.

After going through stages of realizing his old antics of manipulation wouldn't work, Johnny was hit with the fact this stay at Blue Top was different. He needed to change… quickly. But would even changing be enough? Only time would tell.

There would be other meetings between Johnny and his parents, including talking through plate glass windows. Again, there would be lots of tears shed by the three.

"One night, the Holy Spirit went to work and I just got on my knees in my cell," he said. "I said, 'Lord, I've messed up. I need more than just getting out of jail. I need help.'

"There had been a lot of times when I thought when I run out (of meth) this time I'm not gonna do it anymore. This time, I was sure of it."

Chapter 24

———◆———

DAYS OF RECKONING

CHIEF RONNIE WHITWORTH, who'd lived next-door to Percy and Clara Ann Dyess and their sons on Highland Drive, weren't just nearby neighbors, but also very good friends as neighbors in small Southern towns often become.

Whitworth, a fan of the University of Alabama's bitter in-state rival Auburn University, knew Johnny well enough to know he had quite the sports memorabilia collection, even at his new house where Johnny was up to no good. "There's no telling what all of those pictures and signed footballs and other stuff were worth," Whitworth said. "He had all kinds of stuff that was signed… 'Bear' Bryant and all."

Once Johnny had been arrested, Whitworth went to Percy and Clara Ann to deliver the news first- hand. They knew something was wrong in their son's life. They suspected it was a drug problem.

"Like every other parent, they didn't want to realize how bad it was," Whitworth said. "No parent wants to rationalize that there is that big a problem."

How big was the problem?

Whitworth was asked that question regarding Johnny's issue

and where it ranked on a scale of 1 to 10, with 10 being the worst. Whitworth didn't hesitate, saying Johnny's problem was at "Nine."

Whitworth told Percy and Clara Ann he wanted them to wait "a day or two" before talking to their son in jail. "They'd always been real supportive of me and I felt like they trusted me," Whitworth said of the Dyesses. "I went to their house and we talked on their back porch. We talked for a long time. The only way I would say it was straight forward. I told them that Johnny was in a mess. I said I would try to help him in any way I could, but the best thing now was to let him sit there in jail and get that mess out of his system."

Whitworth said he knew the routine and Johnny would soon be pulling at his parents' heart strings, begging them one minute and saying he was being mistreated the next.

"I told them he was fine in jail," Whitworth said. "He had a roof over his head, three meals a day and he was warm. I knew he was going to be OK."

As if on cue, Johnny called his parents.

Johnny recalled being locked up… again.

"Once I was there, the first thing I thought about was 'How can I get out?' I became the greatest con-artist and manipulator," he said. "They gave me a $350,000 cash bond. I knew my parents would have it taken care of for me."

His parents had waited several days, weeks it seemed to Percy and Clara Ann, longer for Johnny. They'd asked Whitworth if they could visit their son. He had agreed. So, they told Johnny during a phone call they'd be coming to visit.

Whitworth set up the meeting.

Percy and Clara Ann would wait for Johnny in the chief's office. A jailer would bring him there.

The jailer said he couldn't find the keys to remove the shackles on Johnny's ankles, but Whitworth said that was policy.

Johnny was told the "lost key" story in hopes of easing his mind.

Nevertheless, he'd be escorted to the office to see his parents while in handcuffs and shackles.

"I told them that when he comes in, don't let what you see bother you," Whitworth said. "First, he's gonna look nasty, but he has soap and water. He's going to have leg irons on and handcuffs. I wasn't going to take them off. It was good because it humbled him a little bit. I closed my office door and walked outside. I hated seeing him locked up, too, but even more so what the drugs had done to him."

Whitworth knew Johnny was someone worth saving, but even a seasoned veteran like himself wondered if it was too late. If nothing else, he hated seeing what the ordeal was doing to Percy and Clara Ann.

When Johnny had left his house under arrest, he did so with his head hanging low. He had to as he was helped into the SUV to be transported to jail. He was lowering his head again as he was escorted back to his cell after meeting with his parents, shuffling out as he had shuffled in due to the restraints. He was embarrassed. He was quiet. He was humiliated.

"It was a very humbling experience to sit by my parents with my hands and feet shackled," Johnny said. "I hate that I put my parents through that. That was one of the hardest things. But, it happened for a reason.

"Luckily, that was my bottom and not six feet under. That's what I tell people. They really were angels that came and saved my life. They just happened to be from The Drug Task Force."

Whitworth knew the survival rate for meth addicts was low. It got progressively lower the longer someone had been a user. "I told his mom and dad that the average person on meth lives around seven years." Upon hearing that, Johnny was almost embarrassed to admit to Whitworth he'd been on the drug about 12 years.

Whitworth had seen people recover from meth, but the number was "maybe two out of thousands."

Percy and Clara Ann were being tested, too, as Whitworth continued to preach "tough love" to them.

Four weeks into his incarceration, Johnny was still trying to manipulate people. He wanted out any way possible. He played sick. Jailers had seen that act before. He tried everything, but no one was buying his antics. True love meant separation, and Whitworth made sure Johnny's parents didn't get reeled into any guilt trips by their son.

Weeks after Johnny's latest incarceration, Percy and Clara Ann couldn't wait any longer. They wanted to get help for their son. Little did they know that Johnny was getting help for others, even behind bars.

Chapter 25

WHO'S SAVING WHO?

A FELLOW INMATE at the Coffee County Jail, just a boy he seemed to Johnny, asked one night as Johnny sat on his bed reading, just what it was he was looking at and how was it keeping him so occupied behind the cell's walls.

Johnny had chosen to go back to the Bible - as Percy and Clara Ann had raised him - that had gathered dust the last couple of decades. Its contents had certainly had been ignored, even if opened on occasion.

The fellow inmate didn't even know what the Bible was, Johnny said, so Johnny explained it to him, prompting the guy to want to know more. Curiosity about a book he knew so little about was pulling the youngster to Johnny. "I didn't know it all, but I got to John 3:16," Johnny said. "I knew about that. He didn't. I knew how to lead him to Christ."

A couple of days passed and the young man visited Johnny again. Johnny was more than happy to share more of the Book and the two sat on the floor and began to read.

One day, while visiting with his parents, a jailer stuck his head inside the door and simply said, "Johnny, if you need help, let me know."

Johnny's curiosity would not let him allow the jailer to leave the room so quickly. "What help?" he asked. "What are you talking about?"

The jailer told Johnny about a place, His Place, in Opelika. As part of Harvest Evangelism, His Place was founded in 1986, and works with helping rehab troubled men through a faith-based program. Johnny listened intently to the jailer, but soon had to return to his cell.

Several days passed. It's not as if Johnny had not been to rehab before, but something sounded different about this place … His Place.

Coffee County Jail Administrator Richard Moss handled the paperwork for Johnny, hopeful he'd be accepted at the Opelika operation that preferred being referred to as a life restoration facility more than a rehab facility.

"I was burning up my lawyer's phone," Johnny said. "He got to where he wouldn't even answer if he saw it was coming from the jail. All of this time, I began to read the Book of John in my Bible."

The Gospel According to John describes both the mystery and identity of Jesus, his nature and origin.

On Wednesday nights at the Coffee County Jail, local pastors visit the inmates, preaching about faith and what it could do for their lives.

Johnny hadn't heard anything regarding his possibility of going to His Place. "I kept waiting to hear something," he said. "One day the paperwork had not gotten to the judge. One day the paperwork didn't get to the district attorney. It was one thing after another."

A typical Wednesday night had passed and the local pastors had come and gone. The following night, Johnny saw them coming into the jail again. Something seemed awry because he'd never seen them come on a Thursday evening.

Johnny and the young inmate looked at each and decided, why not go to the meeting again?

It wasn't like there were many other options available. "We went at it again," Johnny said. "They preached on salvation. We all held hands and said the Lord's Prayer."

Then something truly inspiring for Johnny happened. It happened while the pastors were talking to the inmates.

The young inmate who'd begun reading the Bible with Johnny decided to walk up to the visiting pastors and give his life to Christ. "That boy… that was awesome," Johnny said, recalling how he felt, still feels, that the boy had changed his life even while behind bars.

Inspired, Johnny continued reading his Bible, although he began to wonder if His Place was just a vanishing hope, a mirage of sorts. The pastors visited again on their usual Wednesday night. "After they left, I prayed that when the time (to go to His Place) came I would be ready. I was sure ready."

Yet again, Johnny was inspired. But, another inspiration was on its way.

The very next morning, a Friday, a jailer came to Johnny's cell and said, "Get your stuff. You're going out."

And just like that, Johnny was leaving the county jail. He had been accepted by His Place.

"It was nothing that Johnny did," he said. "It was what the Lord did. God kept me there long enough to see that boy saved."

Chapter 26

HIS PLACE

Dyess family photo
Johnny had a weekend leave from His Place and managed to spend
some time with his aging, yet beloved Cinnamon.

You can call him Rick, or Pastor Rick, or you can just call him The Preacher. Regardless, Rick Hagans is going to pour his heart and soul into everything he can at Harvest Evangelism. His Place is the men's part of the program there, in Opelika, Alabama. Opelika bumps up to Auburn's eastern border and is only about 20 miles from the Georgia state line.

Johnny had been to a rehab or two, staying once for 28 planned days – the days his insurance had covered. It was a small rehab center in a small town in South Alabama. Most importantly, Johnny recalled, it hadn't been Christian-based.

"I'd been in one before," Johnny said. "I went to this one (the small one) after I spent 60 days in jail. They taught you a 12-step program, which may be good for a lot of people but it didn't stick with me. I probably faked my way through them. The main step they miss through the 12-step program is getting Jesus in your life.

"They say you've got to put your faith in a higher power. Some of them call it putting your faith in God, but you can put your faith in a door knob as long as you put your faith in something. It's not based on Jesus Christ. You just put your faith in something and start trying to forgive people, make amends with everything. It's a great theory and there's a faith-based 12-step program based similarly on it, but until I turned to Jesus my life never changed. I'd be in prison, or dead, if I hadn't. I stayed sober about four days while I was there."

Johnny had to check in at the jail as soon as he left the small rehab facility, and when he returned home, he stayed for about four more days. That's when a friend of the family came by the house to see if Johnny wanted to go to work for him in the construction business.

Johnny was soon drinking again and quickly found his way back to a meth pipe. "You'd a thought I would have seen a pattern there, huh," Johnny laughed.

An arrangement had been made to have Percy and Clara Ann drive Johnny to Opelika and Harvest Evangelism. Johnny had been so in-grained in loving the University of Alabama as both a former player and lifelong fan, he wanted nothing to do with the Auburn-Opelika area.

"I had to go to Auburn to get my life straightened out," he said. "I didn't want to go anywhere near Auburn or Opelika. I hated Auburn. I hated everything to do with Auburn, but it was better than jail, I figured."

Hagans pastored at Harvest Evangelism and His Place; he was an Auburn graduate. Coupled with the fact that Johnny had already been subjected to wearing one of Auburn University's official colors – orange – as his county jail attire, Johnny just figured God must either have a great sense of humor or a somewhat different approach to changing Johnny's lifestyle.

"I wore orange every day in jail," Johnny said. "I knew I was in trouble then. God was doing all he could do to break me."

It was late August 2009 when Johnny arrived at His Place. He was cleansed of drugs while in the Coffee County Jail, having only occasional access to cigarettes. Even those were not allowed at His Place.

"(His Place) taught me how to love again, how to forgive and how to ask for forgiveness," Johnny said. "They taught me how to pray again and care for others as much as myself."

Johnny said everything about being hooked on meth "was toxic," and His Place attempted to flush everything about the drug from his mind. The year-long program involved lots of Bible study, working at a thrift store, and going to church seven or eight times a week. "We went three times on Sunday," Johnny said. "That's what it takes. The only recoveries I've seen, Jesus has been involved. Some people may get cleaned, but to have a better life, Jesus has to be there. There are a lot of miserable sober people out there."

Hagans does everything he can on the premises, from being a pastor to "picking up junk," to cooking meals at the facility.

"When you're a faith-based organization, everybody does a little bit of everything," he said. He has been there holding the hand of a grandmother and a mother who had just lost a grandson and son after he'd overdosed. That occasion, Hagans said, was on Mother's Day.

Hagans said his success rate is 100 percent. "Here's why," he said. "God taught us to spread His word. We take guys that may come in two or three times… lawyers, pastors, graveyard workers, all walks. They may not get it until they've done it several times. God didn't call on you to be successful. He called on you to be faithful. We share His love, and that's all that you can do. You can make the numbers look really good, but the truth is only God knows."

Hagans then said he was about to bury a "guy that looked really good" to most people, but the man had issues that few, if any, could see.

Hagans is a big sports fan, but had been hospitalized for 15 months after breaking his back playing football as a ninth-grader. He fought back to run cross country, but could never play football, a sport he loved so much, again. He remembered Johnny providing him with a special gift.

Hagans said, "Johnny once gave me a prayer on a note that 'Bear' Bryant had given him that read: 'This is the beginning of a new day. God has given me this day to use as I will. I can waste it or use it for good. What I do today is very important because I am exchanging a day of my life for it. When tomorrow comes, this day will be gone for-ever, leaving something in its place I have traded for it. I want it to be gain, not loss – good, not evil. Success, not failure in order that I shall not forget the price I paid for it.'

The note now sits on a friend's desk somewhere in North Carolina, Hagans said, as he eventually passed it forward.

Chief Whitworth, also an Auburn fan, said methods His Place used were necessary for Johnny.

"At some rehab facilities, patients are on their own 24 hours after being admitted," Whitworth said. "It's hoped they stick around, but it's not demanded. They don't give you things at His Place. You work for what you get. You wash dishes, you clean floors, you have to attend a service. I guess that's when Johnny was really saved. To begin with, Johnny had to want to get out of jail. Once he did, he obligated himself to get better. And, he became better.

"Johnny is a good person. But, he had lost jobs and other things because of drugs."

He was now found, even if he didn't know where he was going next.

Chapter 27

TIMES SQUARE

Courtesy Times Square Church

Times Square Church in New York City played a major role in the
life restoration of small-town Alabamian Johnny Dyess.

AFTER SPENDING A year at His Place, Johnny and others went on a mission trip to New York City. They'd stay at the home of Earl Stocker,

facilities director at Times Square Church, a giant of a church that had nearly 9,000 people visit during several services each week.

"We took 'em barbecue," Johnny said. "We went to dinner one night and I told Earl my story. He asked what skills I had. I told him I had painted and had done some carpentry. He asked if I would be interested in working as an intern for six months at the church. I prayed about it. I wasn't all that enthused about living in New York, but in the back of my mind I knew I still had charges pending in Coffee County and if I came back I could go back to jail. I had a long list of charges. The uncertainty definitely played a part in my decision."

Johnny took the New York offer in 2010. He stayed there 10 months.

Dave Wilkinson founded Times Square Church in 1987. He was Hagans' spiritual leader, or "father," Hagans said. The two had celebrated Bible study together before his new church began operating. While at Times Square Church, Wilkinson would take in broken men and women in hopes of restoring their lives. Wilkinson began taking those same broken men and women and sometimes sent them to Hagans' facility in Opelika. "That's how the New Yorkers wound up in Alabama," Hagans joked. "It was kind of a trade off because I started sending some people up there."

The South Alabama boy wasn't as out of place as expected.

"They loved (Johnny) up there," Hagans said.

When Johnny had the option of going to work in the maintenance department of the church in a cold, big city, far away from his home – about 1,100 miles – in the warm and small town of Elba, per usual, the options were not appealing. The difference this time? Johnny wanted to go.

Something was driving his motor that the stay in inner-city New York City was part of God's plan, he said, to set him on the right path, even if it had taken a detour he never imagined.

Times Square Church is an inter-denominational church located on West 51st Street in the Theater District of Manhattan. More than

100 nationalities and volunteers from more than 40 ministries gather to worship each week at the massive church that handles everything from giving to the disadvantaged, feeding the homeless in New York City, to staffing an orphanage in South Africa.

Its founder, Wilkinson, died in April 2011

When the church opened, Times Square was at ground zero for the X-rated film industry, strip clubs, prostitution, and drug addiction. Pastor Wilkerson said people in the area were "physically destitute and spiritually dead." The church moved from its original location at The Town Hall to the Nederlander Theatre on 41st Street, and eventually to its current location, the Mark Hellinger Theatre, on 51st Street.

The latter building was originally built by Warner Brothers in 1930 as a movie palace. The Warner Theater, as it was known, was converted into a Broadway venue named the Mark Hellinger Theatre, hosting such notable musicals as My Fair Lady, Jesus Christ Superstar, and the Katherine Hepburn musical "Coco."

The church has six services throughout the week – 10 a.m., 1-3-6 p.m. on Sundays, 7 p.m. on Tuesdays, and 7 p.m. on Fridays.

Among the church's throng of parishioners was Mark Gastineau, former New York Jets' defender, who became a member of the "Sack Exchange." Gastineau, in fact, sang in the choir.

Johnny was "as country as they come," according to Hagans. "Yet, here he was living on Broadway and going to a church with eight or nine thousand people."

Johnny moved an estimated 2,500 chairs each week for the variety of services held in the big church. He swept, mopped, and, among other chores, cleaned toilets.

There'd be no time for the glitz and glamour of Broadway. Johnny was sent to the Big Apple to work, whatever elders needed him, and others in similar predicaments, to do. If it was to move furniture, furniture was moved. If something required painting, it was soon painted. If God needed to be found by people, Times Square Church was there to shine the light.

One of those shining the light on Johnny was a man who'd been in some of the darkest places drugs offered. Earl Stocker had come to TSC from a place few survived for long. His life, and those he would touch years later, would never be the same.

Stocker had originally come to the church as an atheist. A native of Toms River, New Jersey, he could not have been more different than Johnny. In his testimony to TSC, Stocker said he spent the first 47 years of his life pursuing crime, including counterfeiting, loan sharking and any other illegal ways of making money. In fact, Stocker said at 47 he had rarely been legally employed, although he had houses, cars and money.

So deeply "saturated" in the crime culture was Stocker that he said he was numb, completely numb. "I spent a good part of my life looking for that brass ring," he said. "I paid dearly for it because I spent 17 years in some of the toughest penitentiaries in the country. I was in prison with my father, with my uncles. I smuggled cocaine out of South America."

Regardless, Stocker said there was something missing from his life. He knew it. "I was always empty inside, never satisfied," he said. Up to that point, he spent one-third of his life in federal and state prisons for manufacturing and smuggling narcotics.

Stocker said God was foreign to him during those dark days. "I was completely immersed in criminal behavior," he said. He thought his mother and his sisters were not normal since they prayed often for him.

For an extra jolt, Stocker went after some scams because they came with the highest risk.

Through a series of events, Stocker ended up at the Hope Christian Center, a Christian discipleship program for people with life-controlling problems, in the Bronx, where his brother-in-law and a pastor talked him into going because they felt he needed a radical change in his lifestyle.

Stocker figured out of respect for them, he'd go for a few days. "Once there, something began to happen," Stocker said. "I heard the Bible preached and it started to have an effect on me. More and more, the things I thought were not normal, I realized were the truth."

Stocker said God eventually began to create a "clean heart" in him. "Instead of receiving my wish to die, I was reborn," Stocker said. "He has given me a new life I never dreamed of."

Stocker went back to school, was provided with legal employment, and placed in a leadership role at his Times Square Church that allowed him to work with men who had similar backgrounds as his. He has a wife and has custody of a teenage son who also wants to follow Christ. "Now, instead of going out to eat with gangsters, I go out to eat with pastors," he said. "I am a changed man."

Stocker became the facilities director at TSC, which allowed him to meet and impact Johnny's life.

Leaving all preconceptions about the Big Apple back in Alabama, Johnny made the trip. He would return a changed man, just as had his mentor, Stocker.

"It was about turning my life around," Johnny said. "Jesus being involved in it was what changed everything. There's no ifs ands or buts about that. When He opened that door for me to go to New York and just get away from everything down here and being in a setting with the Lord's people and living at that church and being involved at that church at Times Square… it was something. People there were praying for me. They had me involved. We prayed every morning. We had Bible study every morning."

Stocker called it the "miraculous healing of our Lord Jesus Christ." He had been called from "deep bondage" at 47. Johnny was 51 when he went to Times Square Church.

Stocker would play a big role in Johnny's life restoration. "Earl Stocker became my boss in New York," Johnny said. "I talked with Pastor Hagans and Earl a lot."

Hagans knew of Stocker, too

"Earl Stocker had been a guy at Life's doorstep," Hagans said.

"He'd been in a tough lifestyle from Philadelphia and Boston and New York. It was a sad situation, and now he was running the maintenance department and Johnny was working for him at the church."

Stocker believes the restoration was all in God's master plan. "We were created by God and He has His hands on us even when we don't know they're on us," Stocker said. "I was always thinking there's gotta be more, there's gotta be more. Today, I know there is more and his name is Jesus."

Johnny had been just a number before, just another statistic, but he felt something very different at Times Square Church. The church is huge and Johnny met many people during his stay there. Someone – Johnny doesn't remember who – at Times Square Church told him, 'You can do better.' They were right.

The light became brighter to Johnny each day at TSC.

"We had remodeled one of the elder's office and Earl came to me a month or so before I was going to go back home to Elba," Johnny said. "The elder asked me what I was going to do when I went home. That's probably when it really struck me. I said, 'Well, I'm probably going to prison. I've got all these felonies that I've got to answer to.'"

The elder then asked Johnny, "Do you not think your God can do what you say He can do?"

"That really kind of hit me," Johnny said. "I'm thinking, 'Do I really believe God can do anything with this, or do I not? Or, is it left up to some human?'"

Johnny told the church elder, "I truly believe there is nothing that my God can't do. He's all powerful. He can do anything."

The elder replied, "Then you need to start praying for all of those people down there in Coffee County, Alabama. You need to pray for the judge and the court reporter. You need to pray for the district attorney and his secretary. Pray for the judge's secretary. Pray for your lawyer and his secretary. You need to pray for anybody in that judicial system down there in lower Alabama in that 12th District. Anybody that's got anything to do with your case, you need to start lifting them up to the Lord and leave it to Him and stay out of it. If you pray, God will do something powerful for you."

Times Square Church says on its mission statement that it offers a relationship with God through Jesus Christ, beginning with salvation and moving to a newness of life, which can only come through the power of God in a surrendered life.

Johnny had surrendered.

"While in New York, God grabbed a hold of me," Johnny said. "Now, let me tell you, New York was a whole 'nother ballgame. I lived in the church at an apartment in the back. I went up there to paint and whatever else they needed. I had painted an elder's office and put an eggshell finish on it. One of the ladies there with another office said she loved the way it looked. The elder told her she had the same paint, just not the same finish. We had painted the other offices a flat color.

"I told myself that I needed to remember that. God gave me a vision that I needed to paint my life a finish that people wanted and not be like everybody else. It's all about how we finish. I needed to put a finish on my life. I needed an eggshell finish on my life. I'm painting my life every day."

Johnny said when he had made visits home from His Place in Opelika, people noticed a relaxed Johnny. Almost too relaxed, some thought. They would tell Percy and Clara Ann that Johnny didn't seem too worried about everything.

 "Johnny gave it to the Lord," Johnny said, speaking in third person. "He wasn't worried."

Stocker was also an elder in the church, but Johnny said his friend "really had a lot of power with the Lord."

Times Square Church says it is a "Christ-centered worship" church, "a fellowship of believers who are burdened to pray and seek the heart of God."

On one Sunday night at TSC, Johnny was asked to share his story in front of about 2,500 people. Before that moment, he could not recall ever speaking to a group of more than maybe 150.

"They thought I talked funny," Johnny said. "I told them that they were the ones talking funny."

While he'd been at His Place in Opelika, Johnny was able to enjoy his beloved Crimson Tide winning the national championship. While he was in New York, Auburn won the title. "God saved me from all of that abuse I would have gotten back there," he said. "I learned to love people in Auburn, but…" He stopped that thought while sporting a large grin.

Another bi-product of the TSC was Johnny's reinstallation into the life of his stepdaughter, even his ex-wife. "We actually have a good relationship now," Johnny said of Bridgett. "She's grown now but still calls me her Daddy. God actually worked that while I was in New York. When I got my life straightened out she came back in my life."

Lisa is remarried now. Johnny is reborn.

Before Johnny's time was up, waves of emotion poured over him. He was safe, even if a bit out of place in New York. He knew several felony convictions would greet him upon his return to Alabama.

Johnny returned to Elba in April 2011.

Chapter 28

His Choice

His Place had not been Johnny's first rodeo at a rehab. He had attempted to rehab his drug use previously, although His Place was his first faith-based facility… outside of church, of course. As for the New York City experience at Times Square Church, well, that was just about as unique as unique can be.

Johnny was indeed coming home, but at what cost? He had never been to court on any of his previous charges that were plentiful, and the possibility of penalties that went with them could be harsh.

Upon finally returning to Elba, he awaited word on his fate. He believed his past, regardless of the distance he had put between it and his current lifestyle, would force him to pay a debt behind prison walls before all was said and done.

Chief Whitworth, Johnny, Percy and Clara Ann got together and had a property bond set up where Johnny could legally be bonded out.

Johnny even found quick work, in about a month's time, in fact, as a custodian at his family church, Westside Baptist.

But the wait was excruciating. He just knew bad news was waiting to spring upon him. After all, no one could escape his past, could they?

Also, this was Elba, where all his troubles had begun; it wasn't Opelika, and it for damn sure wasn't New York.

"There was a lot of uncertainty legally for me back home," he said. "While I was in New York I just gave it to God."

Now home, Johnny had to give it to the legal system.

He would come home day after day and there'd be no word. No word almost made the wait worse. It was not the proverbial 'no news is good news.' Johnny knew the district attorney would have the final say on his outstanding charges.

About two months after Johnny's return home, he arrived at his house one day and grabbed the mail, as he usually did before heading inside. There it was. There was no mistaking its identity. The envelope had the words 'District Attorney' on its upper left, so Johnny knew the document inside contained what he had been dreading.

Johnny placed the still unopened envelope on top of his dresser. It was a heart-beat moment of 'if it's not opened, it can't happen.' "I had been in trouble so many times," he said. "I knew what that letter was going to be about. I figured it was going to be a list of the charges and when my first court date was going to be. All these two years, this is what I'd been dreading."

He sat in the middle of his living room and began to talk to God.

"I said, 'Now Lord, you showed me You could use me in jail to lead somebody to Your Son,'" Johnny prayed. "'I know You can use me in a prison, and if that's where You need me, I'll go in Your service.' All this was leading up to me having to open that letter. I still didn't know what was in it. I got down on my hands and knees. I told the Lord that all our lives we've heard the saying 'where the rubber meets the road.' That means this is real. It's fixin to happen, one way or another. This is it. I'm either what I say I am or I'm false. I either really believe or I don't believe. There are no ifs, ands or buts about it."

The rubber was meeting the road.

"I said, 'Alright Lord, you've proven to me that You can use me in a jail setting,'" Johnny said. "I think that's why He used me to lead that boy to Christ before I left the Coffee County Jail. He proved to me. That was the first time I ever really accepted that if I went to prison, I'd go to prison and serve my time because I'm definitely guilty. I'll share with people in there what Jesus can do and where He brought me from and out of. 'I'll do Your work in the prison until You want me out.' But, I said, 'Lord, I can't help but believe that through all this and everything that's happened in my life that You've got something better for Johnny Dyess to do for You. Not for Johnny, for the Lord. And whatever that is, wherever You want me to go and share what Your Son did for me, which is dying on the cross, I'll go. If it's to go to a little church on the west side of Alabama, I'll go.'

"It took me a little while, probably 20 minutes, but I still had to open that letter. I was praying the whole time. I said, 'Lord, I'm gonna give You the praise no matter what.' I said, 'If this process with the courts is about to get started, I guess I'm as ready as I'll ever be.'"

Johnny was now two years removed from a life of drugs, removed from that dark world. The light shone on him as he had his life restored at His Place in East Alabama and at Times Square Church in New York City.

He admits the Lord had worked with him non-stop in his last two years, ever since the Angels in Black had visited his home. "The Lord was building up my faith, but I don't know if I was really ready to accept what could happen," he said. "But, I had to, whatever His will was."

He was demon-free. Stating he had not been rehabilitated as much as he was "restored Christian."

Charges had been continued in the legal system while Johnny was out of town because he'd been in the program set by Harvest Evangelism.

Finally, Johnny grabbed the letter and opened it. As he predicted, Johnny saw the list of charges. He began to read the letter.

It read: Mr. Johnny Lamar Dyess, this is to inform you that the following charges have been Nolle Prosequi. Those last two words may have just as well been shouted from the rooftops. "Nolle Prosequi, gone," Johnny said, reliving the moment he'll never forget. It meant the prosecutor had declared he would not proceed with further action against Johnny. The charges had been dropped.

"I got back on that floor and prayed and I thanked the Lord so much," he said. "I said, 'Lord, I thank You because You are the only one that could have done this.' There is no other way this could have happened. He never really gave me a vision that it was going to be anything other than going to prison. It was serious, real serious. I was clean and sober for the first time in 20, maybe 30 years. That year, 2011, was the first time I understood what the consequences would be. I was two years removed from being arrested at my house and I finally get the letter from district attorney."

Johnny credits the work of many – Chief Whitworth, Coffee County Sheriff Dave Sutton, Judge Jeff Kelley, Judge Paul Sherling, District Attorney Tom Anderson, and his attorney, Joe Sawyer.

"I called my lawyer to tell him about the letter and he was like, 'I don't understand.' I said, 'Well, I know why," Johnny said. "'My God can do things you can't do. But I do thank you for everything you've done for me.' There's no other explanation. God intervened. That's why we're sitting here today. Those type charges are not just pushed under the rug. I had a record."

Johnny was saved, again. And, this time, he promised there'd be no need for a trip to New York or Opelika or anywhere other than his church to make sure he stayed on the right path.

Johnny said his trip to Opelika was the beginning of getting his life straightened out. He believes God kept him from going to prison because he had accepted that was likely where he was headed and if so then he would just spread God's message there.

Praying has become the norm for Johnny, but there's nothing routine about it. Each prayer is special in his heart. Today, he takes care of his mother in Elba. He does some custodial work at Westside Baptist Church, and works part-time at the Elba Senior Citizens Center. And, of course, he coaches at his alma mater, Elba High School.

Chapter 29

Sin is a Powerful Desire

Johnny doesn't sugarcoat how meth felt to him. "I liked it. If you're sinning and not enjoying what you're doing, you picked the wrong sin."

Johnny, it appeared, regardless of how wrong it was, picked the right sin. Sin is attracted to a starved will. After the discipline football had provided, Johnny was starving.

He desired meth enough to lose family, friends, careers and self-worth during his dark days behind the drug.

Most sins have practical uses. Drugs for instance, can save people's lives or help them recover from an injury or illness. But, if used outside their designed purpose, they can cause more issues for a person. Take a lawnmower, for instance. While they're great at cutting grass, try cutting your hair with one and the result will be ugly.

Meth has no use other than to add a brief amount of pleasure, all the while destroying people and making what may have seemed a problem much worse... far worse. It's a game of Russian Roulette, and with each high comes the possibility of a last breath.

John 8:34 says: "We are slaves of sin. Sin blinds you and binds you."

Also, Biblically, the Lord said to Cain, "Sin is crouching at your door and it desires to have you." Johnny answered his and welcomed meth with open arms. It took away any resistance he may have once had of straying so far away, driven during his darkest hour to perfect the manufacturing of the drug.

Johnny never rested peacefully, whether it was in a jail cell, on a three-day meth high, or even when he could find rest. He may have slept, but he was far from content. When he awoke, there was always a desire to make more, take more, and whether he realized it, sin more.

In Acts 12, Peter was to be put to death with the sword of King Herod, as he had previously with James, brother of John. But while Herod was awaiting Passover's end to bring Peter to trial, the church prayed mightily for Peter.

On the very night prior to Herod bringing Peter to trial, with the prisoner asleep, bound by two chains and between two of Herod's soldiers along with sentries standing guard at the entrance, an angel of the Lord appeared and shined a light in the cell. The angel awoke Peter, telling him to get up. The chains fell from Peter's wrists. Peter was led from prison, although he thought he was just seeing a vision. As they passed the guards, the iron gate to the city opened. They walked down the street before the angel departed.

Peter finally realized the Lord had sent the angel to rescue him.

It took His Place to make Johnny realize the Lord would rescue him and forgive him of all his sins. The desire had been switched from pleasing himself, with the highs meth provided, to serving God. With God in Johnny's heart, sins lost their impulsive power to dominate him.

When Johnny had led the young man <u>in</u> the Coffee County Jail to be saved, it too resembled a moment in the Bible, "Acts" 25:40, where Paul and Silas had been thrown into prison. They were praying and singing hymns to God when around midnight an earthquake occurred and the foundations of the prison were shaken. The prison doors opened and all prisoners' chains were released. The young man Johnny had helped had been set free.

Sin is most unattractive next to Jesus. Sin, it is said, only becomes attractive if someone doesn't see it as sin. People must surrender their desires and admit to themselves they don't need whatever sin it is; in Johnny's case, meth.

A developed desire for God's heart is what Johnny believes delivered him from the drug. No longer would the wrong desire afflict his life. That sin was dead.

And Johnny is alive.

Chapter 30

COACHING

Dyess family photo
Johnny had his smile back as he celebrates with Elba fans outside of
Bryant-Denny Stadium after the Tigers won the Alabama Class 2A
state championship.

JOHNNY WAS BACK home, and among the plethora of things making him feel whole again was his relationship with his parents, Percy and Clara Ann, and the boys he was privileged to coach as an assistant on the football staff at Elba High School.

Those two loves of Johnny clashed one fall day in 2014.

The Tigers had reached the state championship game in Alabama's Class 2A, despite being one of the smallest schools in the classification. The game would be played at Jordan-Hare Stadium on the campus of Auburn University, just miles down the road from Harvest Evangelism and His Place in Opelika.

That's right, Johnny and the Elba Tigers would be going for it all against Fyffe High School at the home of Johnny's most bitter collegiate rival. Coming to Lee County had opened his eyes, and heart, on his previous trip there.

Heavy on Johnny's mind was not just that his alma mater would be playing for all the marbles against Fyffe, but also his father.

Percy Dyess had not been well for the last couple of years, according to Johnny.

"He never led me astray, never gave me bad advice," Johnny said of his father. "I didn't always take his advice. He had a lot of wisdom about him that I didn't take for a long time. He knew that I loved coaching. When he was sick toward end, I'd visited him. One week we'd been practicing during homecoming week. The team had come over to Enterprise for a movie. I visited him at rehab. He had hurt his back. He asked why I was there. He knew how important being with the team was to me."

Percy would eventually be admitted to the hospital. Again, Johnny visited, and again, Percy lectured his son.

"It was the week of the championship game," Johnny recalled. "He said, 'The boys need you.' I said, 'You need me too.' Him telling me that gave me some peace. I had debated going to Auburn because he was in a hospital and I would be riding off in a school bus."

There was a big send-off in Elba with all the students from high school down to the elementary Tiger fans, as well as fans in town, holding signs and cheering on the Tigers as the buses departed for Auburn.

Johnny rode one of the team's buses. As they arrived in Auburn and he stepped off the bus, Johnny was handed a phone. His father would never leave the hospital. He'd never find out if his son's beloved Tigers would win the state title.

He had passed some time while the Elba team made its trek to Auburn.

Immediately, Johnny was taken by an Elba Police Officer – he joked it was the first time he had ridden in the front seat of a police car – that had followed the buses to Auburn. They traveled to Montgomery where his uncle met them and drove Johnny the rest of the way.

"Daddy had already passed away," Johnny said. "They convinced me to go back to the game. They told me that was where Dad wanted me to be. He was already in heaven by then. I just knew. All this other is just earthly stuff. But he was gone. Coaching is part of my satisfaction. I had a different motivation than anybody else. Mentally, I wasn't there where I should have been in the press box (where he coached). Losing your father the day before the game… it's tough. It gave me a lot of motivation to get back and get that satisfaction the next year."

Johnny said as soon as the horn sounded on Elba's 28-17 loss to Fyffe. He thought of his father. "Immediately," he said.

Johnny calls his job, whatever job he's doing, a blessing. "When I'm cleaning, I find myself praying. I pray for everyone. God has worked with me. He has given me an insight into people. I think about their needs. Look what God has done. It is so awesome."

"I can't change the direction of the wind, but I can adjust my sails to always reach my destination." – Jimmy Dean

Returning to Elba could have posed a problem if Johnny allowed himself to once again be surrounded by the wrong people. But he knew better. He had embedded himself with the church, attending Bible study as much as possible.

He also loved his life as a coach, noting Elba head coach Ed Rigby was a one-of-a-kind boss. Rigby had come to Elba prior to the 2013 season and quickly used Johnny's skills to help mold his winning program. Rigby followed his initial 7-4 campaign at Elba with back-to-back state finals berths – winning the Alabama Class 2A title in 2015. Overall, he compiled a record of 45-9, including 11-3 in the playoffs, after four seasons in Elba.

Johnny had feared the State of Alabama would take away his ability to coach at Elba High, a job he truly loved. He awaited word on whether they would allow him to stay as part of the school, at least in an official capacity.

A letter had come in the mail from the state asking Johnny to respond to all his past felony charges. He figured that was the beginning of the end of his coaching career.

"I went in and talked to Coach Rigby," Johnny said. "I said, 'Buddy, you've been there for me, but this is probably all gonna be over in a couple of weeks.'"

Nevertheless, Johnny grabbed the letter from the state and began writing his response to each felony charge. It took a while.

"I wrote about five pages of responses on paper," he said. "I had to get it notarized, but I wasn't about to try and type all of that back in, so I just took it down to the bank and found the lady that notarizes and handed her the forms."

The woman looked at Johnny and said she'd never been asked to notarize a hand-written document, much less several pages. Johnny responded, "Well, this is gonna be a first for you then, so get to notarizing."

A few days later, Johnny was summoned to the superintendent's office. He figured the state had responded and he was about to be told he had to go. Instead, Superintendent Chresal Threadgill told Johnny, "I don't know what you said to those people at the state but you are here to stay."

All was good, once again, for Johnny. He wanted to make sure it stayed that way.

Regarding old friends that may not have Johnny's best interest at heart, Johnny keeps his distance. "I love 'em," he said, "but I can't put myself in that situation again. When the time comes for you to get out of jail, if you're not scared, you're not ready to get out. You should be scared because all of the stuff that put you in there is still out there."

Johnny said he's made as many amends as possible to people he let down years earlier. "I had so many people praying for me I didn't even realize," he said. "Anybody saying, 'Oh, I ain't hurting nobody as long as I stay to myself,' well, that is just a lie straight from the devil himself."

Sober since July 29, 2009, Johnny hasn't touched anything since. The desire is gone. He makes sure he doesn't go near it. If he knows someone is doing drugs, he simply won't go around them. He has been around people he thought were taking drugs, and at that point he leaves. He won't go around people he knows drink, and he doesn't even like being around people that smoke.

"I just don't go there," he said. "The only time I probably even thought about it was that first year in Opelika. During that time, I guess it happens to most people, you get into these bragging wars how much more things I did than you did. Eventually, you separate yourself from those type people. You give the devil too much credit."

Johnny doesn't hide his past with his players. He addresses it if the situation arises. If he or others in the school see a student headed down the wrong road, Johnny gives them a call. He talks to them. They learn not only of his past, but also his wisdom and where he stands.

"I'm honest with them," he said. "I tell them where I've been and where I could be. If it wasn't for the Grace of God, there's no telling where I'd be. God had to pave a lot of streets and soften a lot of hearts to get me in this position. It took a lot of doin's from a lot of people.

"Coaching, that comes behind Jesus and my family. It's what I really love. Those kids, hopefully I have a positive influence on them, give some insight on what could happen if they don't do what's right or if they do what's right."

Why would the Elba School District hire a guy with Johnny's past?

"They didn't hire the old Johnny," he said. "They hired a different person. I tell you, working with Coach Rigby and that football team has been great. It fills a void that drugs and alcohol once did. I get to know what makes the kids tick to a degree. Teenagers can see through people; if they're real or not. This coaching staff cares. Coach Rigby is topnotch. I have a lot of respect for him."

Today, Johnny takes care of his mother in Elba. He still cleans the church. He coaches. And he prays often.

"My life was a mess," he said. "It's a blessing that I have that job. It took love. When I'm cleaning, I find myself praying. I pray for everyone. God has worked with me. He has given me an insight into people. I think about their needs. Look what God has done. It is so awesome."

At each speaking engagement, Johnny quotes Matthew 17:20: "Because you have so little faith. Truly I tell you, if you have faith as small as a mustard seed, you can say to this mountain, 'Move from here to there,' and it will move. Nothing will be impossible for you." In fact, he used to carry mustard seeds in his pocket to hand out to audience members.

People have forgiven Johnny for his past transgressions, and he's forgiven those that led him down such dirty roads. Perhaps as importantly, Johnny has forgiven himself. "Forgiving, it's a good deal, a big deal," he said. "It's everything. That's what I stand on."

The 2015 season saw Elba miss a second, consecutive unbeaten regular season with a narrow loss to Opp in the regular-season finale. Again, however, the Tigers won four straight to reach the Class 2A title game, this one played at Johnny's old stomping grounds at Bryant-Denny Stadium. The opponent was a familiar one: the Fyffe Red Devils.

This time, Johnny wasn't met with bad news as he exited the bus upon arrival. This time, the Tigers didn't lose a lead. This time, Elba won the state championship, 36-22.

When the final horn sounded, Johnny's thoughts again turned to his father. "Immediately," he said.

"That year we won it, we made some calls that worked," Johnny recalled. "The year before, well, I had a lot of other stuff on my mind. From a mental aspect, the year we won it I was more locked in."

He also remembers Coach Bryant's message on everyone doing their part to make the team succeed.

"That's what we try to teach the kids at Elba: Do what you've got to do and it will make everybody better," he said. "It's the same with life. You do the little things so that the big things take care of themselves. If you do your job, the bills get paid. If you don't, they'll find somebody else that can do your job. Football is the best life-teaching thing I can think of. I like to bring a chain to the players with 11 links. If you cut one link and pull on it what's gonna happen? All 11 have got to do their job. If you're a decoy, try to be the best decoy possible. If your main thing is to make a good fake, carry out a great fake. That's like blocking four people; then others don't have to worry about those guys."

Johnny has shared his story with groups from the Fellowship of Christian Athletes, local schools and churches. He's spoken both in Alabama and Florida about how finding his faith helped him find his life again.

"I've been in jail," he said. "I've been on both sides. When they see somebody that's been there, you can't fool 'em. It's like the kids I coach. You can't fool teenagers. They know if you're real or not. You can act like you care about 'em, but when you leave there and you don't really care, they know it. They know it immediately. You don't fool 'em. I learned that real quick. Young people want to listen. They won't listen to some people, but they'll listen to their football coach. I'm very honest with my players. They know me, they know my background. It's no secret. I don't want it to be a secret to them. You know why? I don't want them to end up where I ended up."

He'd studied communications at the University of Alabama, and Resource Management at the former Troy State University. No college course could have provided the real-life issues he talks about. (Anyone interested in hearing Johnny's testimony can e-mail him at johnny-dyess@troycable.net.)

While speaking to Elba Elementary School's "Too Good for Drugs" program, Johnny asked students if they would walk into a swamp, knowing alligators, snakes and turtles were in it. "No," the children answered collectively. One of them added, "That would kill you." Johnny then told the kids that walking over to drugs would do the same thing.

"It all comes down to the choices we make," he said. "I got off the path and I was going to either end up dead or in jail. We talk about idols, and we put them above God. Maybe during my time at Alabama, I put football above God, maybe because church and God wasn't the cool thing to do in my mind. I am a born-again Christian. All that other stuff has been replaced with Christ in my life. My mind doesn't even turn in those circles anymore. I try to stay in the Bible. That takes all my time and effort.

"The Lord always has me working toward something else. I just share with people what Jesus does. I can tell them everything because He does so much. This is about how Jesus turned my life around."

Turned around indeed.

His church family, many of whom had prayed for him for more than three decades, elected Johnny deacon. One of the highlights of his week is a Wednesday morning Bible study group in Elba.

"I was saved when I was 12," Johnny said. "I think that all this time God had a plan for me. He kept my body and mind safe. Those black SUVs that day, July 29, 2009, they were angels sent by God. I'll never forget that day. I don't want to forget it. It changed my life."

Today, Johnny feels blessed to have the job at Elba High, where he's running backs and defensive backs coach, and officially head groundskeeper for Elba City Schools.

"I pray over the campus every day," Johnny said. "I pray with the football team, sometimes twice a day. I try to set an example. "And all I had to do was have faith in a mustard seed."

Johnny said meth is the work of the Devil, regardless of who makes it, takes it or where it's manufactured.

His former wife and stepdaughter have forgiven him; both came to Percy's funeral.

He is particularly remorseful for what he put Cinnamon through, the arrests, and being moved around from caretaker to caretaker. Chief Whitworth had seen to it the dog was taken care of while Johnny was away in Opelika.

When he left for His Place in Opelika and eventually New York City to Times Square Church, Johnny said leaving Cinnamon behind was painful. "Talk about hurting, now that hurt," he said. "When I got home visits from Opelika, leaving her there hurt. It wasn't fair to her. She hadn't done anything wrong. My mother and Daddy eventually took her into their house. They brought her up there to Opelika to visit me a couple of times. They'd surprise me with her."

Cinnamon passed away at Johnny's bedside at age of 15, two months after Percy Dyess had passed. She lived long enough to see her master safely – and healed -- back home. He had Cinammon, a cow/border collie, bulldog mix, he'd taken care of, for the most part, since she was eight-weeks old, cremated. "She was the greatest non-human companion somebody could ask for. Unconditional love."

Johnny lowered his head as he remembered Cinnamon.

Chapter 31

Upstaging Rudy

Photo by Kyle Mooty

Johnny Dyess now makes many speaking appearances, testifying
how his life was restored from a life of drugs to a life of serving
Jesus Christ.

MARCH 22, 2017, almost 8 years after the SUVs pulled up in his driveway and changed his life forever, Johnny found himself sitting in the Pardon and Parole's Building for the state of Alabama in Montgomery.

It was just a few years earlier, although they seemed to slowly melt toward this day, that Johnny had been told by some guys at the Alabama Family Law Retreat at Orange Beach, Alabama that he was such an inspiration that perhaps one day a pardon for his past felony convictions would be possible.

That night at the Perdido Beach Resort, Johnny was seated at the "special guests" table. He hadn't spoken to judges, officers of the court or others in the legal field outside regarding his litany of legal troubles, but he was about to embark on a career of giving his testimony on how life can get better regardless of how deep in the well someone was at any given time.

The first speaker that night was seated at Johnny's table. Rudy Ruettiger had also been a walk-on, one of the most popular ones in college football history thanks to the movie "Rudy" about his playing days at Notre Dame.

Rudy was inspired after hearing Johnny's story.

Johnny said he was asked to speak, not because of his years as a football player at Alabama, rather to share his story as a meth addict "and what you can go from and to if you trust Jesus and let Him in your life."

The two had shared tales of Notre Dame and Alabama, as well as coaches Ara Parseghian and "Bear" Bryant. While Johnny knew Rudy's story, Rudy would learn of Johnny's life when Johnny followed him at the podium that evening. After all, no movie had detailed Johnny's trials and tribulations.

"I had no idea you had gone through anything like that," Ruettiger told Johnny afterward.

This from Ruettiger, whose 1993 movie had been ranked as one of the Most Inspiring Films of All-Time by the American Film Institute.

On the day of Johnny's speech, an Alabama judge called Johnny asking him to talk to the family of a guy he'd been dealing with in the courts. The guy was headed to prison and the judge wanted Johnny to provide some insight, perhaps enlightenment for the family.

"Like my parents tried to help me time after time after time, his grandfather and family had tried to help him, too," Johnny said. "God hit me with a reality check right then and there. I told those people that night, many of whom were judges and drug court people, they were working with a majority of people that were repeat offenders they had seen over and over again. Like myself, I'm sure some of them cleaned up for a while, then fell back."

The reality check? Johnny had come to the realization he was about to do what God had called him to do, and it was why he was asked to speak before about 500 people this particular weekend in Orange Beach.

"What my recovery is all about is being obedient to His calling," Johnny said, noting he has spoken to young kids and adults in a four-state area since that night at Orange Beach. "I told them that if they knew someone was doing something wrong, don't feel like you're backed into a corner and being a snitch or a tattletale. You will probably be saving his or her life. You can go to coaches, teachers, pastors, parents. If you don't feel comfortable in going by yourself, take someone with you. Maybe if you have a friend with you then you can let them know how concerned you are."

School officials have approached Johnny after some of his speeches and informed him that their students were hanging on to every word he spoke. "I just say what the Lord leads me to say," Johnny said.

What Johnny said at the Alabama Family Law Retreat had many among the large crowd in tears. They gave Johnny a standing ovation, and formed a long line after the banquet to talk and shake hands with him. "He was unbelievable," said Wally Lowery, Director of the Alabama Judicial College, about Johnny.

One lady in line asked Johnny to pray for her son. "The hardest thing to do for parents is finally administering that tough love,"

Johnny said. "I told the lady to leave it in God's hands. Had Brother Whitworth not talked my parents out of it, they too would have eventually given in to my con game."

Some of the most powerful people in the Alabama legal system were in attendance that night in Orange Beach, but Johnny left them with words of wisdom regarding how people can indeed change their ways, telling them, "My God can do things you can't do."

Chapter 32

FIRST DOWN

Johnny and his brother, Tim, pose in front of the statue of Paul
"Bear" Bryant on the campus of the University of Alabama.

"God laid the foundation and I am still working on the building."
– Mavis Staples

THEY SAY THE black hole in our atmosphere sucks in its surroundings and whatever enters is never to be seen or heard from again. NASA needn't spend billions researching the black hole anymore because there is a man who has entered it and lived to tell about it.

The long-awaited answer regarding Johnny's pardon finally had a date: March 22, 2017. Chief Whitworth received the notice from the Alabama Board of Pardons informing him Johnny was set to meet before the board on that Wednesday. Whitworth couldn't wait to head home and show it to his longtime neighbor, Clara Ann Dyess, Johnny's mother, who for the last two-plus years, had been a widow.

When Whitworth arrived on Highland Drive, he found Clara Ann on the ground. Now quite aged, she'd fallen and had yet to pick herself up. Whitworth not only lifted her off the ground, but also quickly lifted her spirits with news of Johnny's scheduled appearance in Montgomery. Whitworth told her this was usually done only for those that would indeed be pardoned. While it was not definite, there was reason for optimism.

After standing on her feet and hearing Whitworth's message, Clara Ann told the Chief, "Well, this was worth falling down for."

Johnny had waited since 2013 for the possibility of a pardon. A judge or two had told him they would do what they could following his speaking engagement at the Alabama Family Law Retreat. Months passed, then years. Johnny wondered if it had all been just words. But, he kept the faith.

Early on March 22, an anxious Johnny was driven to Montgomery to the Pardons & Parole Department where parking is very limited. Elba High head football coach Ed Rigby was the driver, and he was forced to park several blocks away, even though they'd arrived quite early for the scheduled 9 a.m. opening.

Rigby believed in his assistant as if he were a member of his immediate family. Rigby had coached in Louisiana, and even a large school in Pensacola, Florida, but had taken the Elba job to be close to his wife Chanda's coaching duties as head women's basketball coach at Troy University.

Johnny and Rigby were also joined in Montgomery by two other friends and the four of them sat in the waiting room with about 100 others, mostly parolees and their family members. Sitting on the opposite side of the hearing room were individuals wishing to speak against those on hand seeking to receive a pardon or parole.

No one was there to speak against Johnny, although he joked the man he had hit twice that day in his Camaro when he was just 19 could be over there waiting to tell just what a dangerous guy was "ole Johnny Dyess." It was one of the lighter moments in the lengthy wait where Alabama football and other time-passing options were discussed.

Changing to a far more serious matter, Johnny wondered if he could forgive someone, no matter how many years had passed, if he'd been the one who had a loved one killed, perhaps in a wreck by someone that was drunk or high on drugs.

"The Bible tells us to forgive," Johnny said. "But, it'd be hard. What would it take? How long is long enough?"

Johnny found himself giving an impromptu testimony to a group of people who'd driven from Florida that sat just one row behind him. They were there to see their son, their grandson, their brother. He, too, had found himself addicted to drugs. They wondered aloud to Johnny if their loved one would ever find a way to kick the habit that had cost him almost everything to this point

"People at that hearing, that's the same look I've seen," Johnny said, looking off in the distance as if wondering how he'd hurt so many friends and family members in his past.

Every walk of life was in the crowd that day. It was a melting pot of human cultures, young, old, poor and financially secure. They all shared the common bond of either having a substance problem or having a loved one with such a problem.

"Who else in that room had people praying for them like I had?" Johnny wondered. "I'd say not many. Anything is possible if Jesus is involved. What if I'd stayed up in my cell with that young man instead of going down to the meeting that Thursday night? Would he have gone and given his life to Christ?"

Though Johnny had arrived early, he was still number 23 on the call list. Proceedings began on time at 9 a.m. but some cases took longer than others. That would be a blessing to the group from Florida as they listened intently to the guy they'd only met some 10 minutes earlier.

Johnny explained why he was there, summarizing his life in a matter of maybe five minutes. The group wanted to know what could be done for their loved one.

"I was broken, but I was willin' to go," Johnny told them. "You've got to want to do it. If He'll do it for me, He'll do it for you. But you've gotta want it."

The "He" of whom Johnny spoke was God, Johnny explained.

"In life, you'll have your back up against the wall many times," Johnny said. "You might as well get used to it."

Johnny described how he dove over his head into the drug world. "You get consumed by it," he said. "I even found myself in a warehouse in Atlanta where I was holding a gun in case anything went wrong with my partner. It makes you make bad decisions. I started making it. Every waking hour – and there were a lot of waking hours – I was either cooking it, making it, using it, or getting up to do it all again. I thought meth was the cure for all my problems. I didn't drink anymore; didn't want to because all I wanted was meth."

The people told Johnny their loved one was only 25-years-old and they worried if he would ever get off meth.

"I was 49 when they got me," Johnny said, recalling the day of the Black Angels. "Don't ever give up. I know it's hard, but don't ever give up. It was not a rehab that I went to, but a life restoration that saved me. It restored my whole life for me. You're never out from it, but you learn to stay away from it."

Of course, changing his life also meant changing his inner circle. Johnny warned of such people that don't have your best interest at heart. "We've all got our go-to people," he said. "I really wasn't selling it, but if I needed to go get some things to help make it, I had people I could go to."

It was obvious Johnny had touched the people behind him that Wednesday morning. It was nearing the noon hour and Johnny and his guests figured he would have to wait until after lunch to stand before the board. Just then his name was called.

Johnny sprung to his feet. His friends followed and his new friends, those from Florida that had listened to all of Johnny's advice, cheered as if they'd known him for many years, wishing him good luck as he walked toward the hearing room.

Many people, including Coach Rigby, Chief Whitworth and Pastor Ken Wilson of Westside Baptist had written character references for Johnny in hopes he'd indeed be pardoned for his past crimes. It would still be up to people who didn't know him, certainly not the man he'd become.

Johnny and his spokesperson, Rigby, sat up front while his other two friends took seats on the second row. The four would be the only people in the room aside from the three board members – a man and two women.

Johnny was asked to approach the podium. He would be the first to speak. He thanked the board for giving him the opportunity to address them. He came across as sincere as one could, even if a little nervous.

He spoke about how the angels in black, the SUVs, were the beginning of the end of his wayward ways. Johnny noted he hadn't touched a drop of alcohol or taken any illegal drug since that summer day in 2009.

However, one of the members of the board noticed the year 2011 on his record. She asked Johnny about the date. Johnny quickly advised the woman 2011 was the year charges were filed, and explained he'd spent 2009, '10 and '11 either in jail, at His Place, or working at Times

Square Church in New York City. "I have not had anything since 2009 and now speak against drugs all over the southeast, "Johnny said.

The woman was satisfied with Johnny's answer.

Rigby was then asked to speak on Johnny's behalf. He talked of being Johnny's friend since arriving in Elba in 2013. "Johnny Dyess makes me a better person when I'm coaching," Rigby said.

Rigby went on to give the equivalent of a pre-game pep-talk to the board.

Rigby had made his point. Johnny was a solid member of society and wasn't a threat to himself or others, Rigby believed he was a true asset to Elba's school system.

"To sit there and watch him and listen to him tell that board about me… wow," Johnny said.

Rigby had been so engaging he was asked how his teams have done at Elba, to which he proudly related they'd lost in the state championship game in 2014 and won it all in 2015.

Shortly after the football comments, a board member looked at Johnny and said, "Mr. Dyess, we are granting you a full pardon."

Johnny later quipped, "I knew we had them when they asked about our football team."

Johnny was arrested that summer day in 2009 on his front porch and his long road to being released from the grips of methamphetamine began. On this day, he was returned whatever freedoms he'd lost along the way.

At 59, Johnny now had his previous acts forgiven, restoring his civil rights to work without having to fill out the line admitting he had, in fact, been convicted of a felony. Johnny can also now hunt. He'd missed hunting almost as much as anything; convicted felons can't legally possess a firearm.

It's a pretty good deal, being a sinner and then forgiven. Johnny smiled: "Yes, it is."

Does Johnny still know how to cook meth? Probably not, passing off the question as if it wouldn't matter if he did.

Johnny said that memory has been erased. "I basically flushed that out of my mind," he said. "I don't even ponder it. I don't think I could remember it if I had to. I hope not."

Drugs were the worst hit he ever received, much harder than the one Sherman Wilkinson handed him as he came across the line carrying the football all those years ago.

Returning to the correct huddle?

Ha! Johnny didn't even return to the correct lifestyle.

Today, Johnny acknowledges the many bad choices he made that led him to the most humbling of moments. He remembers well the date, July 29, 2009, as the day angels came for him in the form of dark vehicles.

And today, Johnny understands all things Auburn are not bad.

Johnny doesn't stay in his house; instead, he spends the days taking care of his mother at her home. Too many ghosts, it seems, at his house. He doesn't even go back in his mind to days when everything centered around meth. "Reminisce? Not so much," he said.

Johnny attends more Crimson Tide festivities as a member of the A Club, enjoying taking people to games to meet people and show them all the pictures of legendary players and coaches.

"I enjoy that," he said with that big Johnny Dyess grin. "It's tough now because I teach Sunday school, have church and on Sunday afternoons and I have coaches' meetings during the season."

But this day was different as he recalled what all he'd gone through, what he'd experienced on his road to Montgomery, where all his past transgressions were wiped off the record

"I learned you can care about somebody that maybe has different alliances. I don't have the hatred for Auburn as I once did. For a long time, if Alabama didn't win it was the end of world. I know it's not now. I witnessed the Kick 6 (Auburn's return of a missed field goal for a game-winning touchdown against Alabama in 2013). I can probably handle anything they throw at me. In 2009, I was in Opelika when Alabama won it all. In 2010, I was in New York when Auburn won the title. God kinda smiled on me through that situation.

"Just having new teeth, I think the Lord took care of all that because He had a plan for me. I think He knew there was gonna come a time where He was gonna have to intervene. I wasn't going to come out of it on my own."

Somewhere in Johnny's mind, he truly believed he was not like the others. Even arrest after arrest, loss of career-potential jobs, slamming of cell doors behind him, and embarrassment he carried from disappointing his parents worse than any nightmare he'd sweated through, Johnny still thought he was different. Turns out, he was right. It just took him the better part of two decades to prove it.

The drug loved him like his best friend, only it was truly the worst acquaintance Johnny could have made. Only meth had no idea of the caliber of what was thumping in Johnny's chest.

Pastor Rick Hagans maintains contact with Johnny, his friend. Johnny has visited him on occasion at Harvest Evangelism. It's not a debt he owes, but thanks for which he can never give enough.

Hagans said Johnny is special to him in so many ways.

"Without men like Johnny Dyess… well, you need a guy like him because God changed him," Hagans said. "God did that. It was a miracle. Yeah, we had people spend time with him, but God did that. We all love hearing in his testimonies how God does change people. I am so proud of him."

Hagans still jokes about the ribbing with Johnny, even during life restoration days at His Place. "I'm an Auburn graduate," Hagans said. "Johnny is always flashing those rings he has from Alabama. He was a mess."

Johnny also has a new perspective on Auburn. Oh, he still loves Alabama and isn't fond of its rival, but things are different.

"At the time I grew up, it was hardcore," Johnny said. "You were either Alabama or Auburn. I don't look at things from an athletic perspective as much now because I have a lot of friends in Auburn. It's a good school. With the shambles my life was in at the time, I can't imagine anybody loving me any more than the people did there.

"My goal now is to have a better relationship with my Lord and savior Jesus Christ and to treat people the way I would want to be treated. If not for Him, you'd have to be interviewing me at a state prison."

He knows that everyone – the late Coach Bryant, Chief Deputy Whitworth, Pastor Hagans, Earl Stocker and many others he met along his road to recovery, and of course his parents – are proud of where Johnny is now with his life, his faith. He knows the way people around him carried themselves were life lessons practically slapping him in the face.

"It was tough on my parents, but they never gave up on me," he said. "I had lost it all because of drugs. I lost my job because of poor job performance, but my poor job performance was because of drugs."

Johnny's brother, Tim, is seven years his junior. "He saw some of what was going on with me," Johnny said. "It hasn't been good in the long run for him either."

Johnny said his message is to never give up on people. He noted Chief Deputy Whitworth never gave up on him, even when Whitworth had asked his parents to show tough love and let Johnny be sent away without bailing him out… again.

Speaking to groups, some churches and countless impressionable high school kids, has become the norm for Johnny.

"I've had Johnny talk to certain people," Chief Whitworth said. "He tells me that some people he can't talk to because the urge would just be too strong; maybe they're old running mates. But, I see him every Sunday in church. He's active. There's never a Sunday that he does not come by and shake my hand. And every time I get around his Mom, she thanks me.

"The guy played football for 'Bear' and had a good job. Those are things people dream of, and now he is settling for groundskeeper and helping with the football team. He works with youngsters and Fellowship of Christian Athletes. He accepts his fate because he knows he messed up. He accepts what he once was, so, he does not complain. To me, he's on top of the world… and, he can never go back."

Johnny realizes he needs to stay there rather than go down again. He's likely out of second chances.

Yet, the final words he was told in the Pardon's board room were "full pardon."

Regardless of who had a hand in it, the ball is in Johnny's court from here on, although he'll tell you he has the best teammate possible.

Former college basketball star Chris Herren, now a motivational speaker, also became addicted to drugs. He would understand Johnny's story. His professional basketball career was cut short because of his drug use. He hit rock bottom several times, even being found passed out in alleys.

In an ESPN documentary on his struggles, Herren said he had been "to hell and back. I lived the life that most people, a lot of people, don't get a chance to come out of, straight up. By the grace of God and the help from a plethora of people, I was able to come out of this."

How many times will a parachute continue to open for someone if, time after time, it is abused? He had chased so often what he believed to be the bread of life, and for that he came oh so close to becoming toast.

"God keeps opening doors," Johnny said. "He did his part, now I'm just trying to do mine. If it wasn't for His grace I'd be in prison. That's where I should be right now. You should be getting a special pass to come to prison to talk to me. I was arrested in 2009, so I'd probably still be in there. Grace is for what you don't deserve. Mercy is for what you deserve. It is because of Jesus Christ that I'm here today."

Johnny's judgment day will have to wait. He's got other matters to tend to.

Among his problems today are bees that have taken up in the building behind the house his parents had purchased for him. It's the building where he became a master chef of methamphetamine.

He still has the house, but he doesn't stay there with all the ghosts, and of course, there are too many bees. He no longer looks at his coins, and besides, times have changed. "It's funny, but old pennies now are from the seventies. Back then, I was looking for the fifties and sixties."

Hugs overrode handshakes among the friends both before and after they exited the Pardon & Parole board room.

"Daddy would be so proud of that pardon," he said. "God did it. He did this. That's the only answer."

"Scooter" Dyess certainly is proud of his nephew.

"Johnny's done so well," 'Scooter' said. "You gotta want it… and Johnny did."

It was lunchtime and that's where the group was headed, a barbecue icon in Alabama named Dreamland.

Johnny was certainly in dreamland. After all, he'd been served a new set of downs.

Even the effects meth left on his body can't stop him from spreading the word today. With his new set of chompers, Johnny enjoyed the barbecue that day. During a reflective moment, he said, "I lost my teeth, but my smile has been restored."

ABOUT THE AUTHOR

Kyle Mooty

Mooty is an 82-time winner of various press association honors in different time zones and vastly different climates. He now serves his dual role as general manager of the Eufaula (Alabama) Tribune and editor of The Enterprise (Alabama) Ledger with the BH Media Group.

Courtesy Henry Otto/Creative Media Images
Author Kyle Mooty and Johnny Dyess moments after the Elba Tigers won the Alabama Class 2A state football championship at Bryant-Denny Stadium in Tuscaloosa.

WHO NEEDED A canine retriever when I was willing to run and grab each dove my father shot in the sorghum fields of west-central Alabama? I would sit there in the high weeds on the field's edge, listening to a battery-powered radio my father always brought to a dove shoot as if it was as necessary as the boxes of shells and the Ithaca pump shotgun he used to down the birds with accuracy unlike anyone I'd ever seen before or after.

Those were some of my fondest memories, sitting in the hot Alabama fall outside on a Saturday afternoon and listening to Alabama games on the AM radio hidden in the weeds. I guess the doves wanted to listen too, just as long as they couldn't see where it was coming from. Between touchdown runs by Johnny Musso or Wilbur Jackson, I'd sprint my skinny rear end out in the field, grab a fallen dove and return it, hopefully before "Bear" Bryant's boys in crimson and white would score again.

I began my newspaper career at the age of 18, again in a retrieving mode. I started on Friday nights, gathering dozens of high school football reports during the late-night and early-morning hours at the *Northwest Arkansas Times* in Fayetteville, Arkansas, where my mother had moved her youngest child after his sophomore year in high school when she became a dean at the University of Arkansas. I had never learned proper typing and during the wee Saturday morning hours I pecked away at the typewriter. Six weeks later, I was offered a full-time position. A once shy teenager, I was coming out of my shell as I learned to talk to strangers, asking those all-important questions about who led the team in rushing and how many times each side had been penalized.

I was raised on "Bear" Bryant and Alabama football, and though I attended the University of Arkansas and bounced around the newspaper business in several states, I kept a watchful eye on the Crimson Tide and called Alabama home regardless of which state I paid taxes. Both of my brothers attended the Tuscaloosa campus, one on a baseball scholarship.

Sports were ingrained in my life, having been the youngest of four of a former college basketball star player and coach – the late Harold Mooty of Centenary College in Shreveport, Louisiana.

I loved all sports, but outside of intramural and softball leagues, I left the playing fields and began a sports writing career shortly after high school. I spent 18 years covering sports from Lou Holtz to Barry Switzer, Gene Stallings and Pat Dye, Eddie Sutton, Wimp Sanderson and Nolan Richardson.

Many years and several states later, I left – some may say I escaped – sports journalism and concentrated more on hard news, as well as running newspapers and magazines from a general manager's post where playing hardball and keeping positive public relations often clashed.

My favorite quote comes from a close friend in the newspaper business who often said, "The role of a newspaper is to be a watchdog for the community… and sometimes we bark."

I ventured into other media outlets, including radio talk shows, business writing and eventually as editor and general manager of several newspapers and magazines across the south and southwest. When I had the opportunity to return to Alabama in 2013, I jumped at the chance, taking a post as editor at Southeast Alabama's *Enterprise Ledger*. Two years later, I took on a dual role as general manager of the *Eufaula* (Alabama) *Tribune* on the Georgia line while maintaining oversight of the Enterprise newsroom.

It was while living in Enterprise that I had a chance to meet Johnny Dyess. I was working on a series regarding the problem with methamphetamine in America. It was not unlike similar articles I had written in other states. I had long since been soured by much of the things I had seen during my career covering everything from killers to spoiled athletes. I'd become as accustomed to interviewing county jail inmates awaiting a bed at the state prison as I had wide-eyed high school kids who had their minds set on becoming the next Michael Jordan or Joe Montana.

One thing that was universal in every town I'd worked was the problem of methamphetamine. A local chief deputy of a sheriff's office had set up the meeting. Johnny agreed to meet me for a review of what had taken the former football player from a small-town hero to big-time college athletics, down a destructive trail holding hands with the most powerful of drugs, and amazingly back into society's safe arms thanks to a faith that had been reborn. I knew I had come across someone whose story was perhaps more special than anything I'd come across in my decades in the media business. When Johnny asked me to pray with him before our first interview, I admit that there was some skepticism because I had seen more drug busts and fatalities than I care to remember, as well as more than my share of drug addicts telling whatever story a reporter wanted to hear. After all, everyone professed their innocence behind bars. Nevertheless, there was something different, very different about Johnny, and it soon had me wanting to break with tradition and telling him just how special the talk had meant on a personal level. By the time Johnny walked out of my office that day, I truly cared for him as if I'd known him since Little League.

I too had dealt with demons of sorts, having been the youngest of four children that had experienced the worst of an alcoholic father's sickness as his years wasted away.

More than a year later, after Johnny had become a hot ticket on the speaking circuit at high schools, clubs, and even a state legal convention, I decided it was time to make the story into a book for more than just readers in his neck of the woods to see. Ironically, on the day I was set to call my new friend to discuss the idea, Johnny came into my office, unannounced, saying he hadn't touched base in a while and wanted to see how his friend was doing. "Have a seat, Johnny," I said. "I have something to talk to you about."

Johnny often talks about how God made this and that happen in his life. For me, it appeared the intuition of writing a book about Johnny's journey down the road to self-destruction and back to a life of clarity was decided by someone with much more powers than any editor or publisher, or even "Bear" Bryant, could have mustered.

I've covered more than my share of sports heroes from the college and professional ranks during my time, but many of those stories ended on the playing fields. With Johnny, the real story was far away from the gridiron.

~~

CPSIA information can be obtained
at www.ICGtesting.com
Printed in the USA
LVHW07*1051010318
568278LV00002B/3/P